Lead your
family in worship

Discovering the enjoyment of God

Francois Carr

© Day One Publications 2008
First Edition 2008

Unless otherwise indicated, Scripture quotations are from the New King James Version (NKJV)®. Copyright © 1982 by Thomas Nelson, Inc. Used by permission. All rights reserved.

British Library Cataloguing in Publication Data available

ISBN 978-1-84625-128-3

Published by Day One Publications
Ryelands Road, Leominster, HR6 8NZ

☎ 01568 613 740
FAX: 01568 611 473
email—sales@dayone.co.uk
web site—www.dayone.co.uk

Cover designed by Wayne McMaster and printed by Gutenberg Press, Malta

Endorsements:

Anyone who knows Francois Carr quickly recognizes two things: he has a heart for his family and he longs for revival. In this helpful work, Francois combines the two. A heart for God is learned at home. Holiness is taught at home. If there is to be revival in our lands and if there are to be great men and women of God leading our churches, then Christian parents must take seriously their calling to raise up a godly generation in their homes. This work will be a great help to those parents seeking to build homes that honour God.

Dr Richard Blackaby
Director of Blackaby Ministries, Canada, and author of several books including the best-selling Experiencing God

I believe that Francois Carr has brought to us a very practical and helpful tool for families. As the family is so under attack these days, we are seeking for things to bring stability back to the family. The essential role of the Word of God must once again become paramount.

Revd John McGregor
Executive director, Canadian Revival Fellowship, Canada

Probably one of the most neglected areas in Christian parenting is that of family worship. Francois Carr speaks of this subject that needs to be addressed in every Christian home and church. This book may sting with conviction, But I am sure it will encourage you in this most needy area of building Christian homes.

Mark D. Partin
Pastor, Indiana Avenue Baptist Church, USA

Francois Carr reminds us of some of the spiritual nuts and bolts that help hold the Christian family together and provide an atmosphere of ongoing devotion in the home. A timely reminder to all Christians who take the spiritual development of their children seriously.

Kevin Adams
Pastor and author of Diary of Revival

Here is an important, timely and scriptural exhortation, and introduction, to family worship. Read and pray over its contents and the Lord can use it to bless your family and also your church. I commend this little book to you.

Dr Eryl Davies
Former principal, Wales Evangelical School of Theology (formerly Evangelical Theological College of Wales)

The Bible clearly instructs families to gather together for biblical teaching and worship. The author's burden is that this vital practice be retained, restored or, in many cases, instituted for the first time. Family worship is essential and Francois Carr is convinced of its merits. He instructs most helpfully in great practical detail how each family can begin worship together in the home. I commend this awakening call with its clear instructions to the Christian public.

Dr Colin Peckham
Former principal, Faith Mission Bible School, Edinburgh, Scotland

It is an old but good saying that families which pray together stay together. This refreshingly up-to-date book on family worship is a valuable contribution to a much-neglected area of Christian practice. May God be pleased to bless its teaching to many.

Revd Maurice Roberts
Minister, Free Church of Scotland Continuing, Inverness, Scotland

Francois Carr has given us a much-needed book on a matter which is being neglected to the detriment of healthy family life. Here is an incentive and a corrective which if read and applied will bring help and healing to families where the family altar needs to be strengthened or restored. This book, if carefully read and heeded, will revolutionize hearts and homes for the glory of God.

Revd Martin Holdt
Pastor, Constantia Baptist Church, Pretoria, South Africa

The issue raised by Francois touches the very heart of discipleship, and the spiritual responsibility of every parent with regard to the family. It is not just a good idea to have family devotions, it is essential. The person who neglects this impoverishes not only his own life, but also the life of his or her family.

Dr Bennie Mostert
Director of Jericho Walls International, South Africa

The words of the Lord Jesus, 'Let the little children come unto me, and forbid them not', are still of relevance today, especially when we see the turmoil in the lives of young and old people from broken families. This book by Francois Carr fulfils an urgent need. I trust that it will be read, assimilated and applied by everyone who comes across it.

Dr Harold Peasley
Director of Multi Ministries International, South Africa

Contents

Introduction

My most vivid and meaningful memories of visiting my grandparents as a young boy are those of being able to join my grandfather in the vestry before walking into the church on Sundays. He always gave me some sweets during the service. I remember the cookie jar with the special treats in the room next to the kitchen, and how all the grandchildren frequently visited it. But I also remember how my grandfather and grandmother would gather the family together after our evening meal and take down the old Bible and read a passage from it. Once the Word of God was read, my grandfather would pray for us. The Bible was alive for him.

When I think of my father, I remember how he helped me and my sister to memorize Psalm 23. We saw him read his Bible every night and bow his head in silent prayer. In the last few years before his death, he would always insist that we read and prayed together before we went to bed at night. These are memories which I can never forget—memories that have helped to shape my life and which are, I believe, probably the greatest heritage that my grandparents and parents could possibly have given me. This is what I would like to leave behind as a spiritual legacy to my family.

Christians whose homes used to resound with the sound of hymn-singing and prayer before the day began now start the day with rush and hurry. Some years, ago the Queen broadcast a message to the women of the British Empire. Among the excellent things she said was this:

> It does seem to me that, if the years to come are to see some real spiritual recovery, the women of our nation must be deeply concerned with religion, and our homes are the very place it should start. It is the creative and dynamic power of Christianity which can help us carry the moral responsibilities which history is placing on our shoulders. If our home can be truly Christian, then the influence of that spirit will assuredly spread through all the aspects of our common life, industrial, social and political.[1]

We hear much about revival these days, but it is always in connection with the church. I believe that all churches and congregations wish to experience growth: growth in their membership, growth in their church structures, growth in their finances, growth in missionary and outreach programmes, as well as spiritual growth through enjoying intimacy with

God. The implementation of special projects and techniques in order to achieve these objectives is widespread. While I agree that each of these objectives does contribute positively to the life of the church, it seems that these special projects haven't brought about a major breakthrough nor any lasting and positive change in our society.

We all long for a positive change, especially in our countries, communities and local churches. Church groups and denominations constitute the community of believers. Churches consist of families—and families consist of individuals. Yet I have visited and preached in numerous congregations over the years and have found few that have focused their growth, and more specifically their spiritual growth, on the foundation of the righteousness and holiness of individuals and family members. The root of a healthy spiritual life and growth is a revival in the heart of an individual that has a visible impact on the family. If a family is spiritually healthy, it leads to spontaneous growth in the church and to further spiritual development of the community.

The well-known American lecturer and writer Revd Theodor Cuyler rightly said,

> For one, I care little for the government which presides at Washington, in comparison with the government which rules the millions of American homes. No administration can seriously harm us if our home life is pure, frugal, and Godly. No statesmanship or legislation can save us, if our homes become the abode of ignorance or the nestling of profligacy. The home rules the nation. If the home is demoralized, it will ruin it. The real seed corn whence our Republic sprang was the Christian households represented in the 'Mayflower', or the family altar of the Hollander and the Huguenot. All our best characters, best legislation, best institutions, and best Church life were cradled in those early homes. They were the taproot of the Republic, and of the American Churches.[2]

I wonder if perhaps God is saying to us, 'You're working in the wrong place.' Ask God to bring revival in the home. If he does, I guarantee that it will infect the church. And I believe that it begins when you and I establish as a priority a daily system to meet the spiritual needs of our families.

1 A forgotten command of God

Therefore you shall lay up these words of mine in your heart and in your soul, and bind them as a sign on your hand, and they shall be as frontlets between your eyes. You shall teach them to your children, speaking of them when you sit in your house, when you walk by the way, when you lie down, and when you rise up. And you shall write them on the doorposts of your house and on your gates, that your days and the days of your children may be multiplied in the land of which the LORD swore to your fathers to give them, like the days of the heavens above the earth.

Deut. 11:18–21; also read Deut. 6:6–10

In the book of Deuteronomy, Moses gave a short and concise description of what happened to the Israelites in the desert. He was speaking to the people of Israel just after they had come out of Egypt and while they were in the valley east of the river Jordan, in the desert, on the first day of the eleventh month in the fortieth year. He gave them the law just as the Lord had commanded him. The Lord cautioned his people to keep and obey his laws, to abstain from idolatry and to love him. He promised them several blessings in return for their obedience, but also set forth a punishment and a curse if they abandoned his laws and were disobedient. His commandments were aimed at leading, protecting and ultimately blessing his people. His commands have not changed, therefore we too have to love the Lord always, and obey all his laws always, not only on Sundays or when we feel like it. He expects obedience from us. 'Therefore you shall love the LORD your God, and keep His charge, His statutes, His judgments, and His commandments always' (Deut. 11:1).

In Deuteronomy 11:18–21, the Lord God gives a specific command to his people. The command is given and addressed directly to the head of a family. (Usually the father represents his family as head; however, if the father is no longer alive, the mother is considered to be head of that family.) The command affects the head of the family, his family members and especially his children and offspring. However, in our generation the command is not obeyed; it is not even simply forgotten, but has to be revived and taught again to all our children.

The spiritual teaching and education of our children has to take place in the home. Children have to be brought up in a loving and godly atmosphere, where the family worships God, obeys his commandments and walks in his ways. Obviously this is to take place daily and be an ongoing process. According to Deuteronomy 11:18–21, it should take place when we sit down, when we are at home or travelling, when we lie down and rest, or when we get up and work. These activities should be observed by all the members of a family. The education of our families should take place in the intimacy and security of our homes. The Lord God wants to be part of our families. The Lord God expects from us that the words of his statutes will be made known to our family members. What is meant by 'these words of mine' (v. 18) and 'when you walk by the way' (v. 19)?

It is clear that the 'words of mine' refer to the words that have just been spoken. God's words to the people (and the family) are his laws and his commandments, as given through his servant Moses, which he expects us to obey and carry out. The Hebrew word translated 'way' in verse 19 (and also Deut. 6:7—*dhelerith*) indicates 'way of life', 'manner of conduct', 'action' and 'daily walk'. The laws and statutes of the Lord are there to show God's children how they are to live their daily lives and how they should act towards one another and towards God. He is not only interested in our obedience to his laws and regulations, but he also wants to be involved in all our daily activities. He is our God, longing for an intimate relationship with each one of us.

We read about the same command and challenge in Luke 3:4–6:

> as it is written in the book of the words of Isaiah the prophet, saying:
> 'The voice of one crying in the wilderness:
> Prepare the way of the LORD;
> Make His paths straight.
> Every valley shall be filled
> And every mountain and hill brought low;
> The crooked places shall be made straight
> And the rough ways smooth;
> And all flesh shall see the salvation of God.'

Here the Greek word translated 'way' and 'road' is *hodos*. It carries the same meaning as *dhelerith* and could be understood to mean the way we live, act and interact with one another, even referring to our everyday journey through this life.

In Luke we have a clear command from the Lord to prepare and smooth his way. If we do that, the end result will be that all mankind will see God's salvation—the Lord Jesus. We read the words of Simeon, when he took the child Jesus in his arms in the temple:

> Lord, now You are letting Your servant depart in peace,
> According to Your word;
> For my eyes have seen Your salvation
> Which You have prepared before the face of all peoples,
> A light to bring revelation to the Gentiles,
> And the glory of Your people Israel
>
> Luke 2:29–32

'Your salvation' refers to the Lord Jesus. In the New Testament, God commands us to conduct ourselves and interact with one another in our daily lives in such a way that all people will see the Lord Jesus in and through us. We read that the Lord Jesus is the way and the truth and the life (John 14:6). He is the true way of God. He is also the true Word (John 1), and his words are the commandments of the Lord God; 'If you abide in Me, and My words abide in you, you will ask what you desire, and it shall be done for you' (John 15:7). God gives a clear command to his people. He wants to be part of our daily activities and lives. He wishes for us to live in such a way that the whole world will see his Son, the Lord Jesus, in and through us. The Lord Jesus will become visible in the way we deal with one another and in our relationship with him. Family worship, the spiritual education of our family, should be a way of life.

It is clear from these passages in the Scriptures that the Lord wants us to understand and obey his words, statutes and commandments. Furthermore he wants to be personally involved in our lives. God wants to bless each one of us, and I believe that everyone wishes to see and experience the blessings of the Lord God. His condition—and the only condition—is that we obey and carry out his commands daily. Furthermore, he desires that this special relationship with him be lived out particularly in the privacy of our homes and in the spiritual education of our children. When we obey his commands and live in a relationship with him, the Lord Jesus becomes visible in our daily lives.

A HOLY LIFE

Helen Ewan, a Scottish girl from Glasgow, died in 1932 at the age of twenty-two. She was an ordinary, everyday Christian, yet also an extraordinary one. Her daily routine and life were filled with the glory and presence of God. She spread the fragrance of the Lord Jesus wherever she went and had a marked influence on the people she encountered. As a young adult she spent hours each day reading the Bible and praying. She believed the words of Robert Murray McCheyne: 'It is the look that saves, but it is the gaze that sanctifies.'[3] Helen gazed with rapture into the face of her Lord. Her life made such an impact on others that hundreds attended her funeral.

Helen had been encouraged by the example of her parents. The Lord Jesus was the pivot around which the whole existence of the family revolved. James Stewart, a family friend and her biographer, was touched and challenged by her life and example. In his book *She Was Only 22*, he relates that he always saw three worn Bibles on the table of the living room when he visited them. Helen Ewan's parents were poor, but left a rich legacy:

> Although she died at the age of 22, all Scotland wept. I know hundreds of missionaries all over the world wept and mourned for her. She had mastered the Russian language and was expecting to labor for God in Europe. She had no outstanding personality; she never wrote a book, nor composed a hymn; she was not a preacher and never traveled more than 200 miles from her home. But when she died people wrote about her life story. Although she died so early in life she had led a great multitude to Jesus Christ.
>
> She arose early each morning at about 5 o'clock to study God's word, to commune, and to pray. She prayed for hundreds of missionaries. Her mother showed me her diary—one of her diaries—and there were at least 300 different missionaries for whom she was praying. It showed how God had burdened that young heart with a ministry of prayer. She had the date when she started to pray for a request and then the date when God answered her petition. She had a dynamic prayer life that moved God and moved

man. I was talking one day with two university professors in London City. We were talking about dynamic Christianity, when one of them suddenly said, 'Brother Stewart, I want to tell you a story.' And then he told me that in Glasgow University there was a remarkable young lady, who, wherever she went on that campus, she left the fragrance of Christ behind her.

For example, if the students were telling dirty stories, someone would say, 'Sh-h-h, Helen is coming—quiet.' And then she passed by and unconsciously left the power behind her.

The University professor told me how in their prayer meetings they could always tell when this young lady entered the room. She did not even have to take part in prayer. The moment she entered the room, the whole of the meeting was revolutionized by the mighty power of God. 'And,' said that professor, 'she led many of those students to Jesus Christ.' She was the greatest power for God that he ever knew in his life.

I said, 'Sir, that could only be one person. That was Helen Ewan.' He said that was the name of the young lady. I have been out on the streets of Glasgow at midnight, in the awful cold winter night giving out tracts and doing personal soul winning, and as I have been going home, I have seen Helen Ewan with her arms around a poor, drunken harlot, and telling her of Jesus and His love.

Friends, she led a great multitude to Jesus Christ. And when I went years later to the place of her burial, one of the grave diggers said, 'Preacher, I'll never forget when that young lady was buried here. When I was burying that body, I felt the presence of God all over this place.'

One night we were all having a social evening together, young people rejoicing in the Lord, and having a good time, when my wife said, 'Is that Helen Ewan's photograph on the mantlepiece?'

Suddenly there was a dead silence and she said, 'Jim, have I said anything wrong?' All the laughter ceased and one by one, without a word, we dropped down on our knees and began to pray!

Think of it, years after she had gone home to heaven, her name was so magical and so powerful. Oh, friends, I believe that this spiritual life is for every child of God![4]

The life of Helen Ewan, and the effect it had, was the blessed fruit of the spiritual and godly family where the Lord Jesus took the place of honour and where family worship—a hidden treasure of God's blessings—was practised.

For many years, we as parents have left the spiritual education of our children in the hands of the authorities in schools and in the church. But our school curricula have changed and Bible teaching is no longer part of them. In addition, membership of churches is dwindling and some churches have discontinued child and youth programmes. It was never the intention of God that the school and church should educate our children spiritually. God's command was given to the parents, but we as parents have disobeyed the command and the responsibility.

This disobedience was through convenience, but we are now beginning to see its effect in the lives of our children and families—lives that don't reflect the Lord Jesus. Sadly, family worship, the spiritual education of our children, has become a forgotten command of the Lord God.

Summary

- God gives us certain commands.
- God promises to bless us as families.
- God expects obedience in return.
- God wants to be personally involved with each one of us.
- The spiritual education of our children is the parents' responsibility.
- Spiritual education has to be part of our daily routine at home.
- Spiritual education prepares the way for Jesus.
- Family worship should be a way of life.
- Family worship is a forgotten command of the Lord.

2 Why is family worship necessary?

Stand in the ways and see, and ask for the old paths, where the good way is, and walk in it; then you will find rest for your souls.

Jer. 6:16

The best investments are those that are safe and permanent. If we are wise, we will spend our time preparing for that which lasts for ever. What is life but preparation for eternity?

Bishop J. C. Ryle, the famous Church of England clergyman and first bishop of Liverpool, made this enlightening comment when thirty-nine years of age and a father of five children:

> It is not enough to keep boys and girls at home and shut out every outward temptation. They carry within them a heart ready for any sin, and until that heart is changed, they are not safe whatever we do. Bad companions are a great evil to be avoided as much as possible. If parents were half as diligent in praying for their children's conversion as they are in keeping them from bad company, their children would turn out far better than they do.[5]

Every parent needs to ensure that family worship is restored and revived again. But why is it so important and necessary for us as parents to see to it that our families, and especially our children, are spiritually educated?

God expects that from us

First of all, it is a direct command from God. We have seen that in Deuteronomy 11:18–21 the Lord God commands his people to *teach* their children and their offspring. It is a clear command to all families—and to the extended family. It affects all the family members in the home, especially the children, as well as other descendants, such as our grandchildren. They have to be taught according to the commands and the ways of our Lord.

It serves to prevent backsliding

The spiritual education of our families serves as a countermeasure to backsliding and turning our backs against God. Leonard Ravenhill, a noted American minister and writer, once remarked, 'As goes the church, so goes the world, and as goes the world, so goes the church.'[6]

Church history shows that the church has had a visible influence and impact upon communities and the world, especially in times of revival and spiritual awakenings. Revival in the church has even brought about changes in secular social structures and the Reformation.

However, it is also true that few or no real changes take place when spiritual apathy, self-righteousness and worldliness take hold in the church. The church then visibly loses its grip on the sinful practices and wickedness of society.

In my home country of South Africa, there are currently some 3,000 denominations and 34,000 churches; yet there is no real noticeable change in society. Every year the number of church members declines, and churches are merging.

The 'powerlessness' of the church is evident. It seems as if there is no real lasting breakthrough despite all the efforts of our churches.

Why is the spiritual life of so many at such a low ebb? Why are our nations and countries so unfaithful to the Lord? Why is it that there is such a tremendous rise in wickedness, godlessness and sinful practices? Why are so many of our churches empty and some almost spiritually dead? Why is the spirituality of so many of our families just an empty façade?

The words of the Lord Jesus in the book of Matthew are becoming more appropriate every day: 'And because lawlessness will abound, the love of many will grow cold' (Matt. 24:12).

Evil seems to be on the increase daily. The media bombards society on all levels with sex, violence, pornography and such things. What the media offers is worsening daily, increasingly pushing the moral boundaries and becoming morally destructive. Religion plays no part in what the media offers and therefore appears to be powerless. Everything appears to be a frenzied search after power, violence and recognition. Unrighteousness is on the increase and Christians seemingly do nothing about it. Things that were earlier seen as sinful and frowned upon by society are becoming everyday practice within the family and church today.

As a result, the love of many believers is growing cold; increasingly, we justify these things that are accepted and practised by everybody. We say we needn't be so conservative and legalistic. Complacency, self-indulgence and the cooling of our love of the Lord (spiritual backsliding) result from such an attitude. In 2 Timothy 3:1–5 it is described like this:

> But know this, that in the last days perilous times will come: For men will be lovers of themselves, lovers of money, boasters, proud, blasphemers, disobedient to parents, unthankful, unholy, unloving, unforgiving, slanderers, without self-control, brutal, despisers of good, traitors, headstrong, haughty, lovers of pleasure rather than lovers of God, having a form of godliness but denying its power. And from such people turn away!

The congregation of the church consists of a greater or smaller number of families. The spirituality of the individual has a marked effect on the spirituality of the family. The spiritual family in turn has an impact on the congregation. The spirituality of the church has a significant effect on society and makes a mark in the world. Someone once said, 'The way things are in the home is the way things are in the church and in the world.'

At the end of his life and 'ministry', Joshua addressed the people for the last time with these words:

> And if it seems evil to you to serve the LORD, choose for yourselves this day whom you will serve, whether the gods which your fathers served that were on the other side of the River, or the gods of the Amorites, in whose land you dwell. But as for me and my house, we will serve the LORD.'
>
> Josh. 24:15

With these words, Joshua confirmed his commitment as an individual, and that of his family, to the Lord. The people of Israel then committed themselves to God, made an offering and called the place Bochim (Judg. 2:5). Then all the people returned to their own parts of the land. The people of Israel served the Lord as long as Joshua lived and during the time of the leaders who came after him (Judg. 2:7). After those leaders died, however, a generation (children and grandchildren) rose up that did not know the Lord and his works. They stopped worshipping the Lord and began to serve other gods (Judg. 2:10–12). Surely this is confirmation of the need for parents to bring up their children in the ways of the Lord.

In 1966, Richard Lyon Morgan, professor in theology, highlighted the same tendency and problems in an article in the *Herald of Holiness*. (Today, nearly forty years later, the situation has deteriorated even further.) Prof. Morgan carried out his research at a Christian college, questioning 150 first-year students. The questionnaire consisted of twenty-five easy questions, such as: Where was Jesus born? Which is the first of the Gospels? Who was Moses' successor? One student mentioned that, although he had attended Sunday school, he couldn't remember anything of what he had learned. The average mark was only 10%; the highest score was 34%, and two-thirds of the questions were left unanswered.

The answers were appalling. Some thought that the Ten Commandments were given by Jesus on the Mount of Olives, that Jesus was born in Rome and that he was baptized by John in the Red Sea.[7]

Lack of biblical knowledge in society as a whole is obvious today, but the biblical literacy of the current generation in the church is also at an alarmingly low level. Although there may be outward signs of spirituality, and some churches may even have grown in membership and the number of buildings they own, there is a real lack of eagerness and commitment to read and obey God's Word. It is clear that Christianity is only one generation away from spiritual backsliding and total biblical illiteracy. If we do not familiarize our young people with biblical truths and teach them to walk with the Lord Jesus, the next generation will not be Christian.

Joshua's life, and the example he set, ensured that his own direct descendants remained in contact with God. If we ensure that our own loved ones, children and their offspring, are God-fearing, we can empower the next generation to continue following him and not to forget or forsake him. If each and every churchgoer walks with the Lord Jesus and leads his or her family spiritually, it should serve as a powerful defence against spiritual backsliding throughout society.

Spiritual welfare of our loved ones

'Only a disciple can make a disciple' (A. W. Tozer).[8] Spiritual education in the home is an investment not only in the spiritual welfare of our children, but also in the future and continued existence of the Christian faith in our country.

A REVIVAL PREACHER

During the years 1880–1887, God mightily used Richard Owen, a Welsh revival preacher. His life and ministry were later regarded as preparation for the Welsh Revival in 1904. He preached in the northern parts of Wales and touched the lives of around 13,000 people who came to Christ through his preaching. His name was well known by the time of his death at the age of forty-eight. To study his life and ministry grips the soul.

What touched his life and changed it? His parents and the godly atmosphere in their home had the biggest influence on his life. His father was a farmer on the island of Anglesey and died when Richard was only eleven years old.

Family worship, the memorizing of Bible verses and the Christlike gentleness and lovingness of his father impacted profoundly on Richard's life. His father's love for the Lord Jesus, his active prayer life and the exemplary life he led served as grounding for one of the greatest revival preachers in Wales. The ministry of Richard Owen was the blessed fruit of the spiritual and godly family where the Lord Jesus took the place of honour and where family worship—a hidden treasure of God's blessings—was practised.[9]

There is an unmistakable link between the quality of the spiritual lives of our children and our loved ones and the spiritual teaching they have received at home. King Solomon refers to this observable fact in Proverbs 22:6: 'Train up a child in the way he should go, And when he is old he will not depart from it.'

My family and I once watched *Pay It Forward*, a film which tells the story of a boy with a very special school project. He does good to others in the belief that these deeds will eventually reap fruit in the recipients' lives. This is similar to the way in which we should spiritually educate our children. Spiritual education is an investment by parents in the hope that their children will continue to serve the Lord once they have left home.

Jonathan Edwards is considered by many to be America's greatest theologian and most profound philosophical mind. He is noted particularly for his leadership in the Great Awakening of 1740–1742, America's first major revival. He followed in the footsteps of his famous grandfather, the Revd Solomon Stoddard. His life and work had a tremendous effect on the community of Northampton, Massachusetts. On one occasion, he remarked,

> Let me now therefore, once more, before I finally cease to speak to this congregation, repeat, and earnestly press the counsel which I have often urged on the heads of families, while I was their pastor, to great painfulness in teaching, warning, and directing their children; bringing them up in the training and admonition of the Lord; beginning early, where there is yet opportunity, and maintaining constant diligence in labours of this kind.[10]

One source of Edwards' family's stability and legacy was the steady, dependable routine of prayers that they had together, before breakfast and again after supper. Edwards clearly believed in preparing his family for eternity, leaving a heritage that still affects Christendom more than 300 years later. By the year 1900, the marriage and family of Jonathan and Sarah had produced:

- 13 college presidents
- 65 professors
- 100 lawyers, and a dean of an outstanding law school
- 30 judges
- 66 physicians
- 80 holders of public office, including three US senators, mayors, governors and a US vice-president
- 135 books written and 18 journals and periodicals edited by members of the family.

They entered the ministry in platoons and sent 100 missionaries overseas, as well as stocking many mission boards with lay trustees.[11] The spiritual education of our children and families is a crucial building block of the church, community and future.

The spiritual influence of parents isn't always very noticeable. Young people go through different phases and are subject to peer pressure. Some are swept along and land in sinful practices. Not a single family is safeguarded from that. Other children leave the home rebelling against the spiritual education of their parents or their parents' expectations of them to attend church and Sunday school. Some 'suffer' the spiritual education patiently, only to break away completely from any spiritual education or contact with spiritual things once they have left home.

Yet it is often the upright and noble example of parents which restrains children from serious sinful practices. The image of a mother kneeling in prayer may be used by the Holy Spirit to restrain a child from falling into serious sin.

Charles Spurgeon, that prince of preachers, and minister of the well-known Metropolitan Tabernacle in London, once told of the tears and prayers of his mother. She prayed, 'Lord, Thou knowest if these prayers are not answered in Charles's conversion, these very prayers will bear testimony against him in the Judgment day.' His mother's prayer gripped his heart and kept him from continuing in sin. He remarked, 'The very thought that my mother's prayers would serve as witness against me in the Day of Judgment sent terror into my heart.'[12]

The story of the prodigal son in Luke 15 is a good example of a young man breaking away from his father's home. He sold his property and wasted all his money in reckless living with his friends. After he had spent everything and had nothing left, he remembered his father's love and returned to him. Spiritual education at home is an investment in the spiritual welfare of our loved ones. There may not be immediate results, but remember that the Word of the Lord 'shall not return to [him] void' (Isa. 55:11).

Summary

- Spiritual education is a command of God.
- The spiritual life of the individual has an influence on the family.
- The spiritual life of the family has an influence on the church.
- The spiritual life of the church has an influence on the community.
- Family worship serves as a defence against spiritual backsliding.
- Spiritual education is a spiritual investment.
- Spiritual education serves as a foundation for the future of the Christian faith.

3 Why is family worship necessary? (continued)

The most important factor for the emotional adjustment and well-being of a child is the emotional climate in his home.[13]

Clyde Narramore

Family worship is one of the most lasting and effective tools for training our children in the nurture and admonition of the Lord Jesus and preparing them for eternity. Sadly, it is today one of the most neglected disciplines of the Christian life. Although attending Sunday school and church are fine supplements, they are no substitute for the parent's responsibility and commitment to prepare an emotional and godly atmosphere in the home.

Andrew Murray, author of the classic work *With Christ in the School of Prayer*, had praying parents. They not only had regular family devotions, but they also interceded daily for each of their eleven children. In addition, Murray's father, while living in Graaff Reinet, South Africa, spent every Friday evening praying for revival in the church and worldwide. Murray remembered standing outside the study door listening to his father crying out to God and pleading for an outpouring of the Holy Spirit. Little did Andrew Murray know that he would be instrumental in being part of the answer to his father's prayers.

Benjamin Wadsworth stated that every Christian should do all he or she can to promote the glory of God and the welfare of others; and the maintenance of family worship in particular families tends to promote these things.[14]

We have seen already that God expects us to have family worship, that it serves to prevent us from backsliding and that it also lays the foundations for the spiritual welfare of our families. I can think of a number of other, practical reasons for having family worship:

- It gives parents a daily opportunity to model humble dependence upon God.
- It ensures daily intercessory prayer on behalf of our family's needs.

- ✦ It provides a daily setting for reading and instruction from the Bible.
- ✦ It provides a forum for reinforcing the memorization of the fixed forms of public worship.
- ✦ It draws the family together at least once daily—no mean achievement in today's hectic and fragmented world.

But it is also important because:

It gives us a clear conscience

Paul said that he had lived with a perfectly clear conscience (Acts 23:1) and that he did his best always to have a clear conscience before God (Acts 24:16). Spiritual education in the home establishes the way for us to stand before God one day with a clear conscience concerning the spiritual teaching and welfare of our loved ones. Each one of us is destined to die and to be judged by God (Heb. 9:27). Unbelievers and those who are indifferent to the Word, whose names aren't written in the Book of Life, will appear before the white throne and be judged (Rev. 20:11–15). Believers, whose names are written in the Book of Life, will appear before the judgement seat of Christ and be judged as believers. We read in 2 Corinthians 5:10, 'For we must all appear before the judgment seat of Christ, that each one may receive the things done in the body, according to what he has done, whether good or bad.'

We will have to answer for what we have done in our earthly lives—whether good or bad. The Lord God will examine:

- ✦ Our relationship with him and his Son, Jesus Christ. Have we accepted his Son as our Saviour and Redeemer, and did we keep his commandments?
- ✦ Our relationship with our neighbours. Have we reached out to them and served them?
- ✦ Our relationship and response to the Great Commission.

The Lord expects us as parents to obey God in taking charge of preparing our families for eternity. There is nothing so heart-rending as being uncertain about the ultimate destiny of our children, especially if we haven't guided them and we know it; or if we know that their blood may some day be on our hands before the Lord God.

J. C. Ryle once remarked, 'Happy indeed is the father who can say with Robert Bolton on his deathbed to his children: "I do believe that not one of you will dare to meet me at the tribunal of Christ in an unregenerate state".'[15] Can we say today with a clear and undefiled conscience that we have done everything possible to ensure that our loved ones and children revere God and will be with Jesus for eternity?

I was recently in England on a preaching tour. While there I saw a photograph of a twelve-year-old girl and her mother on the front page of a local newspaper. The girl was holding a baby—her own baby—in her arms. She was one of 499 children in England who, at the age of twelve, had given birth to a baby. Her mother wasn't worried as much about the baby as about the fact that both she and the girl were apparently unlucky in their love relationships. They had chosen the wrong partners. Is it possible that we are losing our perspective of eternity? Is it possible that we are living merely for the pleasure of the moment and for the gratification of the flesh? Is it possible that our priorites have changed?

DAVID AND SOLOMON

King David reigned for many years over Israel. He loved the Lord with all his heart and is particularly remembered for his psalms. However, he will also be remembered for his sin with Bathsheba. David was aware of God's command not to gather horses and multiply silver and gold for himself, and also not to multiply wives, lest his heart be turned away (Deut. 17:14–17). He followed most of this consistently throughout his life, but he multiplied his wives and set a bad example for his sons. It was his love for women that caused him to sin with another man's wife.

King David was painfully aware of the effect on other people of his sin with Bathsheba. So when his son Solomon became king of Israel, David instructed him, 'As for you, my son Solomon, know the God of your father, and serve Him with a loyal heart and with a willing mind; for the LORD searches all hearts and understands all the intent of the thoughts. If you seek Him, He will be found by you; but if you forsake Him, He will cast you off forever' (1 Chr. 28:9).

Solomon loved God, walking in the statutes of his father David (1 Kings 3:3). However, his desire for peace caused him to make many treaties and alliances with surrounding nations, and he took wives as a symbol of those alliances. He took many wives, and they caused his heart to stray from God in later years. Could it be that the sin and example of David played a role in Solomon's love for women?

As parents, we have to live at all times in such a way that our children will never be able to point a finger at us and blame us for not directing them on the straight and narrow way. It is terrible for some parents when their children are indifferent towards the things of the Lord. But it is even more terrible to know that we haven't set a good example and didn't give suitable guidance, and that we are not sure where our children will end up.

It helps to educate our children

The spiritual teaching of our children in the home contributes in a big way to their general education. If children are personally involved in home devotions, it contributes to their overall development. Reading the Word or other passages helps to develop our children's comprehension, concentration and intellectual and mental abilities. The act of discussing things with other family members, along with the discovery of spiritual truths and understanding of how to apply them in practice, increases knowledge and provides practical advice about how to do things in society. Children gain a better grasp of spiritual truths, of how the world works and of how they should behave.

Family worship promotes harmony and unity in the family, particularly when the relevance of Scripture is highlighted in daily living and when, in times of illness, sadness, pain, temptations and even persecution (which occurs in many countries), spiritual lessons are the basis of strength and comfort. The family discusses these aspects and prays about them together, creating unity and a feeling of togetherness. Everybody in the family, and especially the children, is enabled to evaluate and handle these aspects in the light of the Word. Thus, family worship serves as a buffer for the family in facing the onslaughts of life. It prepares children for their future lives awaiting them in the world.

Family worship helps children to develop spiritually and to share their thoughts freely about any spiritual aspect. They learn to read the Bible out loud and to pray in the presence of other people. These abilities make them more confident with school assignments and presentations. Family worship therefore offers the opportunity to be involved in the whole education of our children, not only spiritually and emotionally, but also in preparing them for 'adult' life.

My daughter Leone was recently chosen to be one of the leaders in her grade. One of her responsibilities is to conduct a weekly devotion every Wednesday morning for a Grade 3 class consisting of forty children. I have taught her not to prepare a devotion that will be read to the children but to share something that is living in her heart and which the Lord is teaching her from her daily devotions. It is simply amazing to see and hear how the Lord is speaking to her and to watch her, a thirteen-year-old, gaining confidence and growing spiritually.

It is the best use of time

We live in a time when it seems as if the days are simply rushing past us. I remember vividly the day my daughter was born. I was so excited just to hold her in my arms. I couldn't wait for the day when she would be able to put her little arms around my neck. But it seems as if all this has happened overnight—sooner than I expected it to happen. She is a teenager today and still growing. Before long she will be old enough to go to university and leave the nest to stand on her own two feet. Time flies. There is so little time. It is gone in a flash.

We have our children (if they are spared) only for around eighteen or twenty years as part of our families, in our homes and under our care and guidance. This is the only time that we have to secure their spiritual foundation.

The spiritual education of our children isn't difficult and shouldn't be seen as punishment.

The time that we could spend together as a family, to chat, to pray and to enjoy one another's company, is filled and consumed with so many other activities. School, extra-curricular activities, sports, hobbies, friends and so on—all consume much of our time. Make good use of every opportunity you have, because these are evil days (Eph. 5:16). Don't procrastinate, thinking there is still much time. We have to realize that there is really very little time, and that life is like a puff of smoke. 'Come now, you who say, "Today or tomorrow we will go to such and such a city, spend a year there, buy and sell, and make a profit"; whereas you do not know what will happen tomorrow. For what is your life? It is even a vapour that appears for a little time and then vanishes away' (James 4:13–14).

It prepares our hearts for public worship

In the 1920s, families used to gather around a radio to listen together. In the 1950s, they started to gather around the TV. Today, many families have a radio and TV; kids have stereo systems, iPods or other MP3 players, DVD players, mobile phones and computers. We are living in days of exciting technological advances and progress. In the past, activities were planned around the church, the Bible and family time. We can and are using all these wonderful 'advances' to make the Christian life easier. We can receive a daily devotional text message on our mobiles, devotions in our emails and Bible programmes on our MP3 players, and we are constantly improving our resources, even Christian resources. The sad thing for me is that, with all these tools, we receive hundreds of emails and text messages that bombard us with advertisements to buy new materials and resources. The latest trends are advertised with scantily dressed men and women selling lust, pornography and other worldly things with the latest product. We have become so desensitized to these things that we do not notice any more, or even care. In Matthew 24:12, Jesus said that, due to the increase of unrighteousness, the love of his children would grew cold. Families spend hours watching television, visiting shopping malls and enjoying entertainment, but they cannot spend five minutes together as a family talking about the things that will affect their spiritual lives and walk with God. I believe that the church has largely failed to recognize the 'death' of family worship in our present-day culture. For many people, religious activity takes place only on Sunday, when we are ushered into the presence of God as we gather in public worship. However, spiritual education, or family worship, should not be seen in isolation. Jerry Marcellino explains in his book *Family Worship* that worshipping God happens at three levels. It consists of:

- personal or individual worship
- worship in the family
- public worship in the local church.[16]

We cannot separate our lives from our public worship. God has been pursuing an intimate love relationship with us. He has called us to have communion with his Son, the Lord Jesus (1 Cor. 1:9). As we cultivate our love relationship with him and allow him to change us, the changes become visible to our family members and they see the holiness of our lives. They will see our walk with God and, at the same time, be drawn to experience the same intimacy and joy of walking with him. Our walk with God helps to prepare our hearts for family worship; family worship leads and builds upon our walk with God. If the whole family is taught how to spend some time with God, it creates a wonderfully warm and loving atmosphere in the home. Additionally, it brings a new dimension to our time together as a family. But it also prepares our hearts for public worship. Our own personal quiet times and times of family worship create the opportunity for the Holy Spirit, who lives and dwells within us, to stir our hearts and prepare our hearts to worship together publicly. Public worship then becomes a natural extension of our daily experience of walking with the Lord.

Could it be that the decline of many churches is linked with the death of family worship and not cultivating an intimate relationship with God? Could it be that the deadness or apathy in so many churches may be directly linked to the great number of families who are merely 'Sunday-morning Christians'? Being a Christian and worshipping God, whether privately, in the family or in public, aren't things that you can switch on on Sunday and switch off on Monday; they are part of us, part of a way of life, part of an intimate relationship with Christ. The biggest problem today is the fact that many believers are only Sunday believers. If all individuals and families were to experience an intimate walk with the Lord, it would add much to the spiritual atmosphere during our special times of public worship, and would affect our culture. Family worship prepares us for public worship.

Summary

- We are all destined to die.
- We will all be judged.
- God will evaluate our earthly walks and lives in the home.
- Spiritual education in the home can help prepare our loved ones for eternity.

Chapter 3

- Spiritual education in the home supplies us with a clear conscience.
- Family worship contributes to the education of our children.
- Family worship brings unity and harmony to the family.
- Family worship prepares our children for the onslaughts of the world.
- Time goes by quickly.
- Time is consumed by many activities.
- Time has thus to be set apart for spiritual education.
- Being a Christian is about having a relationship with Christ.
- Family worship brings the family into a daily relationship with Christ.
- Family worship prepares us for public worship.

4 Why don't families worship together any more?

It is highly honourable to family-worship, as a spiritual service, that it languishes and goes into decay in times when error and worldliness make inroads in the Church.[17]

James W. Alexander

The Afrikaans forefathers used to say, 'Let us pray.' Everybody knew that it was then time for family worship. Family devotions (the home altar) were ingrained in their lives and practised every day. I recently saw a photograph in a local newspaper of a well-known person playing a small harmonium. The caption stated that it was the very same harmonium that was used by Paul Kruger, president of the South African Republic in the late nineteenth century, in his daily family devotions. The Bible was a reality in the lives of such forebears and in the lives of their family members. However, this is not so common today. Family worship has almost disappeared and those who practise it are in the minority.

Why don't families worship together any more, and why do we even find direct opposition against it? I believe that many reasons can be singled out for the disappearance of this practice. Too little time and full programmes may well be the most common excuses for not having family devotions. May the prayerful words of the prophet Isaiah come true:

> Oh, that You would rend the heavens!
> That You would come down!
> That the mountains might shake at Your presence—
> As fire burns brushwood,
> As fire causes water to boil—
> To make Your name known to Your adversaries,
> That the nations may tremble at Your presence!
> When You did awesome things for which we did not look,
> You came down,
> The mountains shook at Your presence.

Chapter 4

> For since the beginning of the world
> Men have not heard nor perceived by the ear,
> Nor has the eye seen any God besides You,
> Who acts for the one who waits for Him.
>
> Isa. 64:1–4

Isaiah prays to God, imploring him to open the gates of heaven, to come down and visit his people and bless them. He realizes that everything will change when God comes. Oh, if he would come and bless us! He can change our lives and destinies by a mere word. He can change our families, congregations and countries, if only he would come; but he doesn't. Why, then, isn't he coming?

Isaiah explains that the Lord wants to come, but 'cannot' come. He then states the following reasons why God doesn't come down and bless us:

Sin and unrighteousness of the people

The Lord wants to visit and bless us, but because of our sins he cannot. We read in Isaiah 64:5:

> You meet him who rejoices and does righteousness,
> Who remembers You in Your ways.
> You are indeed angry, for we have sinned—
> In these ways we continue;
> And we need to be saved.

God hates sin. The Lord isn't too weak to save, nor too deaf to hear our calls for help; but our iniquity has become a barrier between God and us, and our sins separate us from God when we try to worship him, so he doesn't hear us (Isa. 59:1–2). We commit two types of sin every day: sins of commission and sins of omission. These are sins that we commit wittingly and even unwittingly.

We read in 1 John 3:22: 'And whatever we ask we receive from Him, because we keep His commandments and do those things that are pleasing in His sight.' It is clear from this that answer to prayer is dependent on our obedience to his commands and instructions. If we do not obey his commands, we are disobedient. Disobedience is sin and this causes God to conceal his face from us; hence he cannot then bless us. We sin when we do not obey his instructions and commands.

But what is the connection to family worship? It is that God commands us to teach his way, and to teach our children in the home (Deut. 11); if we don't do this, we are disobedient, and disobedience is sin. Sometimes sinful practices are carried out in the home, such as cursing, swearing, lies, deceit and worldliness. If we live sinful lives and are disobedient to God, we must appreciate why the Lord doesn't want to help our families, our congregations, our countries or us. Our sins prevent him from doing so.

ELI AND HIS SONS

Hophni and Phinehas were the sons of Eli. They grew up in a godly home. Their father was a priest who stood before the Lord on behalf of the people of Israel. His duty was to serve God, especially the ark of the covenant, which represented the presence of God. These two men experienced the wonderful provision, protection and the very presence of God; however, they did not know the Lord (1 Sam. 2:12). This is shocking! Imagine it: the sons of a priest not knowing God! As they grew up and became priests themselves, they lived corrupt lives, dishonouring God by rejecting the commands and statutes of God. Imagine seeing the very presence of God, standing before him, experiencing his holiness, yet continuing a lifestyle of sin! They turned away from the counsel of the elders and fell deeper into sin. Their corrupt lives had a profound effect on all the people around them.

In his book *Chosen to be God's Prophet*,[18] Dr Henry Blackaby discusses the effect of the sins of the sons of Eli and the cost of their disobedience:

Firstly, their sin affected God. God judged them for their wicked and corrupt lives. They were killed on the same day. Sin cost them their lives (1 Sam. 2:31–34).

Secondly, their sin affected the people of God: 'Therefore the sin of the young men was very great before the Lord, for men abhorred the offering of the LORD' (1 Sam. 2:17). Their sins also affected the elders as they became unfamiliar with God and his ways, not having been taught. The elders in turn led astray God's people, who followed the counsel the elders gave out of their own reasoning. Death and destruction became a part of their destiny, as thousands of people died. The sins of Eli's sons had a profound effect on all the people of God during their lifetime and for generations to come. God always sees our lives in detail, and deals with us accordingly.

Thirdly, their sins affected Eli. God charged Eli with favouring his sons, honouring them 'more than' God (1 Sam. 2:29). The fact that his sons did not know the Lord was due entirely to Eli. Eli was more concerned about his sons' feelings and responses than he was about his responsibility towards God. He did not teach them the ways of the Lord. The fact that the sons were born into the priesthood did not guarantee that they would know God. It was Eli's responsibility to help his sons to have a vital, living and intimate relationship with God, but he failed in this. The priesthood was simply a religious practice for them. Today, churches and families are full of people who are well taught in religious practices but do not have an abiding relationship with Jesus Christ. God judged Eli for this sin.

Fourthly, the sins of Eli and his sons also affected Samuel. Samuel was God's chosen priest and, although he was called by God himself, he too was not a good or godly father (1 Sam. 8:3); the sin of his two sons was the reason for the people of Israel wanting a king instead of having God continue as their King. Could it be that the sins of our children affect the people around us today, and even the futures of our nations?

Self-righteousness and self-justification

Our sins not only prevent God from coming down to us, they also lead us to self-justification. We read in Isaiah 64:6:

> But we are all like an unclean thing.
> And all our righteousnesses are like filthy rags;
> We all fade as a leaf,
> And our iniquities, like the wind,
> Have taken us away.

The phenomenon of self-righteousness and self-justification is probably one of the biggest problems in the church today. This usually results when we are knowingly living in sin but don't want to abstain from or break with it. The sin may be 'too' enjoyable. Then we begin to explain and justify our actions. We find reasons to allow us to carry on, even though God's Word is against it. Self-justification carries us away from the Lord like leaves blown away by the wind. We may even think that we are spiritual, but we fool ourselves. We are lukewarm and not on fire for the Lord. In the book of Revelation, the Lord talks about us being in this spiritual state, where we think that we are right but are not:

I know your works, that you are neither cold nor hot. I could wish you were cold or hot. So then, because you are lukewarm, and neither cold nor hot, I will vomit you out of My mouth. Because you say, 'I am rich, have become wealthy, and have need of nothing'—and do not know that you are wretched, miserable, poor, blind, and naked—I counsel you to buy from Me gold refined in the fire, that you may be rich; and white garments, that you may be clothed, that the shame of your nakedness may not be revealed; and anoint your eyes with eye salve, that you may see.

Rev. 3:15–18

We so easily justify our disobedience and sins committed in the home. It is actually only an excuse for not wanting to obey the Lord's commandments. We do not realize that we have a problem and that we do not experience any real blessings from the Lord. I will discuss some of the most common excuses for not having family devotions in the next chapter. We read in Proverbs 28:13, 'He who covers his sins will not prosper, But whoever confesses and forsakes them will have mercy.'

Our prayerlessness

Sin and self-justification always lead to prayerlessness. We read in Isaiah 64:7:

> And there is no one who calls on Your name,
> Who stirs himself up to take hold of You;
> For you have hidden Your face from us,
> And have consumed us because of our iniquities.

Why are there so few prayers going up? Personal prayers, prayers in family worship and during prayer meetings in churches are on the decline, or even don't exist at all. We have to pour our hearts out before God before he can shower us with blessings. And even when we do pray, we don't see any true breakthroughs. Can it be that we pray without our hearts being in our prayers?

Two principles stand out clearly in the above passage from Isaiah. Firstly, we will only start praying once we realize how desperate our needs, situations and circumstances are. We don't pray and call out to God, cleaving to him, because we are blinded by our sin, our self-righteousness and self-justification. It is as if we do not see the hopelessness of our own circumstances. We justify ourselves. We have created or accepted a Christian life of comfort and self-indulgence rather than one of humility and devotion to Christ.

Secondly, we have to realize that our only hope and solution lies with God. We do not realize this, thinking that we can find solutions on our own, whether they be in terms of finance, new courses or programmes. We fail to recognize that our problem lies with us in our lack of meaningful prayer lives and that, as a result, there can be no meaningful family worship.

Summary

- ◆ God wants to bless us.
- ◆ God cannot bless us because of our sins.
- ◆ Sins obscure the face of the Lord.
- ◆ Sins have to be confessed and repented of.
- ◆ We do not want to break from certain sins and we justify ourselves.
- ◆ Self-righteousness and self-justification are the results of unconfessed sin.
- ◆ Self-justification leads to a formal, cold prayer life.
- ◆ The result is prayerlessness.

5 Common excuses for not having family worship

You must live religion as well as talk religion.[19]

Eleazar Mather

There is a lot of resistance to spiritual education and the practice of family worship. The root of the problem is our own unwillingness to obey God's Word, but we'd rather find excuses and justify ourselves. There are some practical problems militating against the practice of family worship, but they aren't unsurpassable. If the spiritual education of our children is so important to us that it is a priority in our lives, we will try to find practical solutions to our problems.

My family doesn't want to participate

Sometimes one member of the family may wish the family to serve and worship the Lord Jesus together, but the other members are not interested in doing so. It may be that the children resist family worship or create a negative atmosphere with off-putting remarks, facial expressions or body language. If we as parents lead an exemplary life, we fear God and our character is above reproach, we can apply a simple rule when the children are merely rebellious or difficult: 'But as for me and my house, we will serve the LORD' (Josh. 24:15).

Our children are dependent on us for as long as they expect us to care for them in supplying warm beds, a roof over their heads, food to eat, clothes to wear (often expensive clothes according to the latest fashion), an allowance (even to pay for entertaining a girlfriend), use of the family car and payment of school fees. They are thus still under our authority and should respect us as the head of the house—even if this only applies until they leave school, are confirmed in church or leave the home. The following is a simple rule to follow until the time that they leave the home: No family worship, no allowance/food to eat.

It may be a little more complicated if one of the parents isn't interested. But there is no problem too big for the Lord Jesus to solve. It is in his heart and it is his desire that every individual will live in a personal and intimate relationship with him.

If one parent (or both) is indifferent, children can do the following:

- Be faithful in your daily personal quiet times with the Lord.
- Be obedient and submissive to your parents at all times and in all things.
- Be an example to them in spirituality without preaching to them.
- Reach out to them by exercising and living lives of love (1 Cor. 13).
- Ask them spiritual questions and for advice from time to time, even if they cannot answer.
- Ask for permission to go to spiritual activities.
- Pray for your parents every day.

If you are a wife burdened with the desire to have family worship but your husband, the head of the family, is indifferent, you can do the following:

- Be faithful in your daily personal quiet times with the Lord.
- Be an example without preaching (1 Peter 3:1–2).
- Submit to your husband.
- Reach out to him by exercising and living a life of love (1 Cor. 13).
- Ask him spiritual questions and for advice from time to time, even if he cannot answer.
- Pray for him every day.
- If you have children, read to them and pray together with them in their bedrooms, before they go to sleep.

If you are the father, the head of the family, and are truly burdened by the spiritual education of your loved ones, you can do the following:

- Be faithful in your daily personal quiet times with the Lord.
- Be an example and a person of integrity to your family.
- Support your family (1 Peter 3:1–7).
- Reach out to them by exercising and living a life of love (1 Cor. 13).
- You are the head of the home and are under the obligation and

command of the Lord. You have to gather your family together to read and pray. Conduct family worship.

◆ Pray with (if possible) and for your family every day.

There is no time

'We really do not have the time to read and pray together as a family.' This is a general feeling among numerous families. As a family, we may be involved in too many activities that might not be God's will for us. We need to consider prayerfully how to reduce the number of these activities or the time spent on them in order to have more family time to spend with God. It is clear that families who spend many hours just relaxing, browsing in shopping malls or watching television, but do not have time to read and pray, have their priorities all mixed up and wrong. Some families have the appearance of spirituality and godliness, but have rejected the real power of our religion (2 Tim. 3:4–5). Time that we take from our pleasures and private activities is not lost time: it is time that adds to the blessings of God for the family.

There are only the two of us

The family is never too small or too large to spend time together with God. Puritan writer Richard Baxter once remarked, 'A family is created and exists of one person leading and another person being led.'[20] Every believer in the family has the Holy Spirit in his or her heart and as Comforter. The Comforter is a person but also God. Furthermore, the Lord Jesus says in Matthew 18:20, 'For where two or three are gathered together in My name, I am there in the midst of them.' It is important to realize that the Lord Jesus is with us through the indwelling of the Holy Spirit. He is in our midst. No family is too small, since God is with us through his Spirit. We need nothing more.

Summary

- There is substantial resistance to family worship.
- Sometimes just one family member may not be interested.
- Families sometimes don't read and pray together because of lack of time.
- Families are sometimes engaged in too many other activities.

Chapter 5

- ◆ Families have to prioritize.
- ◆ A family is never too small for family worship.

6 How do I prepare myself and my family for family worship?

No man can approach the duty of leading his household in an act of devotion, without solemn reflection on the place which he occupies in regard to them. He is their head. He is such by Divine and unalterable constitution. These are duties and prerogatives which he cannot alienate.[21]

James W. Alexander

We can make certain preparations to ensure that as a family we experience the maximum benefit during the practice of family devotions.

What are my expectations?

It is important for both parents and children to share with one another their expectations and the desired results of family devotions. The expectations may sometimes be so idealistically high that they cannot realistically be attained. This creates unnecessary stress and a sense of guilt for all the members of the family and it results in a tense and reserved atmosphere. The intimacy of family worship may easily be lost through narrow and legalistic rules and regulations.

The opposite is also true. If the standard of spiritual education is weak, it could result in the family having no respect for the head of the family, for spiritual things or for God. The family then lives in an apostate state, which in reality is living in sin, but under the banner of spirituality. We have to consider what we as a family want to accomplish through our spiritual education.

Is it important for me?

It is crucial that we consider the priority of spiritual education. We need to decide what role it will play in our lives. If it takes first place, the members of the family are admitting complete dependence on the Lord in all aspects of their lives. He is not an optional extra, but a vital necessity. The parents must be of one mind about this. If one parent does not fully admit this dependence, spiritual education is unlikely to be seen as a priority.

I believe that all humans on earth have in fact only two groups of ultimate needs. The Lord God created us with a vacuum in our inner being. This vacuum creates a thirst and hunger for something that only he can satisfy. We look to satisfy these needs not through him, however, but through numerous alternatives—even through sin.

The first group of needs consists of a longing for peace, rest and joy, and to know that all our sins are forgiven. When we know this, we find rest for the unrest and vacuum in our souls. The Lord Jesus died on the cross to give us real peace and rest. The Lord Jesus came to fulfil our first set of needs.

The second group of needs is to experience love, acceptance and intimacy in our spiritual lives. The filling with and fullness of the Holy Spirit answers this set of needs, filling the void in our lives. He empowers us to live in victory over sin.

All these needs can be met in the family through spiritual education. We have to be convinced first, though, that we actually have these needs. The conviction in our hearts that family devotions are important will lead to its implementation in our families.

Family worship shouldn't be seen as an additional obligation but a normal, everyday family activity, in the same way that breathing is normal to a human being. This calls for flexibility from the family head and family devotions should be planned with the commitments of the family in mind. They should never be seen as a burden or an obligation, but as part of our daily intimate relationship with the Lord Jesus.

It is important to include the entire family, regardless of the ages of the children. Even if the younger ones cannot understand fully or share effectively, they can still listen and observe. The example set by their parents leaves a lasting impression on them. I still remember Psalm 23 because my father made me memorize it when I was only six years old.

Family worship can be practised by:

- a single parent (Acts 16:1—Timothy came from a multi-cultural family);
- a couple without children;
- a family with children;

◆ older people whose children have left the home.

It is important that the leader should ask for the Lord's blessing in his or her personal quiet time before times of family worship.

What is it all about?

Family worship consists of different parts and it is important to prepare ourselves for it. The main aim is both to read and to give instruction from the Word. We must ensure that there are enough Bibles, song books and other aids for each person to read from, or that we remind each member to bring his or her own books when the family gets together. The presentation and format of family worship will differ from family to family. The following are examples of some compositions of families; it is clear that preparation will differ according to the needs of the group:

◆ you are newly-weds;
◆ your children are still young;
◆ your children are teenagers;
◆ your children are young adults;
◆ you and your spouse are alone;
◆ you, your children and your grandchildren are together.

Where does it usually take place?

'You shall teach them [the words of the LORD] to your children ... when you sit in your house, when you walk by the way, when you lie down, and when you rise up. And you shall write them on the doorposts of your house and on your gates ...' (Deut. 11:19–20). The Lord grants us the freedom to choose where we want to educate our children. It is important that we choose a location where the whole family can read and pray together without interruptions or disturbances. Switch off the mobile phone and take the telephone off the hook for the five to twenty minutes that you are together as a family. Some families find it convenient to gather at the table after a meal; others prefer the comfort of the living room or the more formal atmosphere of a study. The location is determined by each individual family. There are no clear instructions about this. In my family, we use the living room and we keep our Bibles, song books and other spiritual literature there. Family worship can take place wherever

45

we as a family decide is best—it is not the place that is important but the getting together.

Family devotions may even take place outside the home during family holidays—on the beach, in the mountains or at some other lovely spot away from home. It doesn't really matter where family worship takes place. When everyone in the family realizes its importance, the family will ensure that it does indeed take place.

When do we need to get together?

'And these words which I command you today shall be in your heart. You shall teach them diligently to your children, and shall talk of them when you sit in your house, when you walk by the way, when you lie down, and when you rise up' (Deut. 6:6–7). It is clear from these words from Scripture that family devotions do not necessarily take place in a specific place and at a specific time in the home. Spiritual education and worship within a spiritually healthy family should be part of a life where you walk intimately with God every day. That is the ideal, but it isn't achieved overnight. Spiritual growth in the family is closely connected to the personal, intimate relationship with God that each member of the family has.

I have spent time with families who, with each meal, read a full chapter from the Bible and then pray, and additionally spend half an hour after breakfast in worship. This kind of time allocation works for those families who do home schooling, whose children have finished their schooling or where everybody works from the same home and has the same time constraints.

There are those who feel that family worship should take place both in the mornings and in the evenings, because that was the way it was done in Old Testament times. This isn't always possible because of the different programmes and time schedules of the members of the family.

For some families, it is impossible to spend time together in the mornings. A friend of mine starts with his own personal quiet time at 4 am because he has to leave for work at 5.45 am. It obviously isn't practical for him and his family to spend time together in the mornings. It is often better to worship together during the evenings, when the whole family is together. However, even this may become difficult, because so many school activities, sports, exams and even church activities are scheduled to take place after standard working hours.

The 'when' needs to be flexible. The devil will do everything in his power to prevent worship from taking place. The Lord God may allow your family to be tempted, to see if you are really committed. It happens that life brings all sorts of things across our paths to ruffle our feathers and frustrate us. I once led a series of meetings on revival about an hour's drive away from home. My little daughter was supposed to go to bed at 8 pm, but my wife allowed her to stay awake until I came home as she was so intent on our reading together as a family. After the last meeting in the series, I had to pack up the books that had been on display and so arrived home much later. My wife and daughter were in bed, but they weren't yet asleep. They had waited for me and tried to remain awake. I got into bed and we just prayed together; due to the lateness of the hour we did not read, but we went to sleep with perfect peace.

It is indeed possible, and important, to set a time for the family to get together—but remember, there will be occasions when we will have to reschedule our time. Our family time together with the Lord should be defended at all costs.

Quality, not quantity

If our spiritual education is narrow-minded and legalistic, we will, in the long run, be unable to maintain the intimacy of praying together. It is more important to focus on the quality of our time spent as a family with God, in his presence, than on the length of the programme or study that we have to work through. It is no use singing three to five songs and reading and explaining a chapter from the Bible if the children are young and do not comprehend what it is all about. In those circumstances, it is more important to be practical and keep our worship short, and instead get together more often. Nothing prevents us from kneeling at our children's bedsides and praying for them, even after having had family worship. With older children, it may happen that they begin to feel that family worship is a punishment and we may lose them in the process if they develop an aversion to it. The focus must at all times be on intimacy with God and with one another, and on quality of time.

Chapter 6

More frequently

It is better to get together as family for five to ten minutes each day than to try to fit in half an hour or an hour two to three times weekly. James W. Alexander, a Puritan author, wrote an excellent book on the spiritual education of the family. He stated that family worship is the manna that keeps our souls alive, just as the manna that fell in front of the Israelites' tents in the desert kept them alive.[22]

Lead the family devotions with strong conviction that it is a priority, but with a soft, broken and tender heart. Even if tired and exhausted, pray that the Lord will help you not to neglect the devotions but give you strength in your exhaustion.

Summary

- ◆ A family has to consider its expectations of family worship.
- ◆ The standard shouldn't be too high or too low.
- ◆ Spiritual education has to be a priority in the family.
- ◆ A family is dependent on the Lord for all its needs.
- ◆ Spiritual education has to be an everyday activity.
- ◆ Spiritual education can take place anywhere.
- ◆ Spiritual education can take place at any time.
- ◆ Quality is more important than quantity.

7 How do we worship as a family?

Let family worship be short, savoury, simple, plain, tender and heavenly.[23]

Richard Cecil

It is our Christian duty to worship God daily. As we have seen already throughout this book, the Lord expects us to have family worship, educate our families in spiritual things and prepare them for eternity. According to Richard Baxter, a Puritan, the families of Christians should be little churches.[24]

Every day, families assemble to offer God praise for his goodness and love, give thanks for his mercies, to hear and listen to his Word and to ask for his guidance for and blessing and protection upon the family.

Worship, therefore, is a devotional exercise. Family worship that employs the commonly used elements and forms of public worship will hasten and enable active participation among the family at a very young age. This chapter provides an outline of things that you might do, adapting them to the needs of your family: singing, reading, teaching and prayer. By using these elements in daily family worship, you will be providing regular spiritual instruction for your family as well as preparing them for public worship services in the local church.

Singing

The Lord God is worshipped by praise and adoration when the family sings together. The Lord God is lifted up and exalted by our singing, and we as family are edified through it. When we sing together, our songs that are based on the Word build us up and strengthen us. Singing serves as spiritual enlightenment and instruction, and the Holy Spirit can use it to lead and protect us.

Make a joyful shout to God, all the earth!

Sing out the honor of his name;
Make His praise glorious.

> Ps. 66:1–2

I will praise the name of God with a song,
And will magnify Him with thanksgiving.
This also shall please the Lord better than an ox or bull,
Which has horns and hooves.

> Ps. 69:30–31

The voice of rejoicing and salvation
Is in the tents of the righteous;
The right hand of the Lord does valiantly.
The right hand of the Lord is exalted

> Ps. 118:15–16

The above quotations refer to praise, worship and song. We are shown that it is a command to rejoice to the glory of God. The command is given to all lands, nations, families and individuals who read through the Word of God. Our praise, worship and collective singing are there to honour his name, not merely for our enjoyment.

The word 'tents' in the quotation from Psalm 118 comes from the Hebrew *bayith*, which also means a house, home or dwelling place. It tells us that we have to sing and rejoice from our 'tents'. The sound of rejoicing has to come from the 'tent' of the church as well as from the 'tent' of the family. 'Let the word of Christ dwell in you richly in all wisdom, teaching and admonishing one another in psalms and hymns and spiritual songs, singing with grace in your hearts to the Lord' (Col. 3:16).

Some family members have the talent of playing musical instruments. A special atmosphere is created by using instruments and they enhance the quality of the singing. Some may feel that they cannot sing and aren't musical in the least. Fortunately, we have a number of aids today that can be used in our family worship. We can obtain handouts with the words of songs for which the accompanying music is available, for example, on CD. If these aids aren't available to you, you can sing unaccompanied.

It is a good idea to sing frequently the songs that our children are taught in Sunday school. They know them and can sing them with great confidence; they will enjoy the family worship and won't see it as an obligation. It is also good for us as adults to become like little children.

The psalms, hymns and spiritual songs that are used in services can also be sung during home worship. These songs often originated in times of great spiritual revival and are filled with references to the Lord Jesus. We will then be singing songs that were inspired by the Holy Spirit. With a little effort in research, we can tell our children something of how the songs came into being, thereby showing them how our God reaches into the hearts of his people. This interesting background information can be a great blessing to our whole family. And just imagine how the singing of a congregation may improve when family singing improves!

In our singing, we as a family (and extended family) can glorify the name of the Lord. This pleases him and makes him happy (Ps. 69:31–32). Therefore, appointed by God as heads of our families, we as parents have a responsibility and obligation to let our families sing together to the glory of God. He deserves it. Let us praise him together daily.

We have to take the following into account when singing together:

- ◆ Sing with feeling and at the tops of our voices.
- ◆ Sing with conviction, our hearts filled with devotion.
- ◆ Sing psalms and hymns.
- ◆ Sing spiritual songs.

Reading

Spiritual education takes place when the entire family reads the Word together. The Lord God commands all parents, in particular the head of the home, to impress upon the children his Word, especially in the privacy of our homes. This indicates an ongoing daily activity, as Scripture says: we have to teach our children when we are working or when we are resting, when we are awake and even when we move around. It thus refers to an activity that should be in the hearts of parents, a yearning to teach and educate their children according to the Word of God.

> It is written, 'Man shall not live by bread alone, but by every word that proceeds from the mouth of God.'
>
> Matt. 4:4

> And these words which I command you today shall be in your heart. You

> shall teach them diligently to your children, and shall talk of them when you sit in your house, when you walk by the way, when you lie down, and when you rise up.
>
> Deut. 6:6–7; see also Deut. 11:18–19

> And you, fathers, do not provoke your children to wrath, but bring them up in the training and admonition of the Lord.
>
> Eph. 6:4

These verses highlight for us the importance of spiritual education. The Word of God—Christ—must be the focal point of all spiritual teaching. Our motive should be to help our family members develop an abiding love for the Word of God. If a love for the Word of God is kindled in the hearts of our family members, they will spend time reading from it on their own. It will radically change their lives (as it must do ours).

The Word should be read with due reverence. It shouldn't be presented in a boring and legalistic way. The aim isn't to give a lecture or message, but to make time for the family to 'listen' together to the Voice of the Lord. The ultimate goal is to worship the Lord together, to read from his Word and to discern if there is a specific word or message from God to the family.

A PIONEER MISSIONARY

John Paton was a Scottish missionary who worked among the indigenous peoples and cannibals of the New Hebrides. He worked on the islands of Tanna and Aniwa, today known as Vanuatu. He was known as the 'King of the Cannibals'. John built several schools and churches and experienced tremendous spiritual blessing on his work.

He had grown up as one of eleven children in the family's five-roomed cottage in Torthorwald near Dumfries. The middle room of the cottage was his parents' bedroom. And it was also the prayer room.

John's father spent time reading from the Bible and praying in that little room after every meal. Everybody knew that there had to be silence in the house once their father entered the room and shut the door, for he was then 'busy with his God'. The life of the family revolved around the Bible and the worship of the Lord Jesus. They read and prayed together twice daily. It didn't matter how busy they were or if guests arrived: they always made time to pray together as family.

John later stated that the example and prayer life of his father was one of the reasons why he went to the missionary field. His father would come out of the little room on many a morning with a shining and sparkling face. His father made this incredible impact on him when John was only six years old. John Paton's life and ministry in the New Hebrides were the blessed fruit of a spiritual and godly family where the Lord Jesus took the place of honour and where family worship—a hidden treasure of God's blessings—was practised.[25]

The Bible is the primary source from which to read and instruct. We may, however, be creative in the daily presentation and reading of parts of Scripture. For example, read the same passage from different Bible translations. It may be a great blessing to the family if different translations are used. If you are reading a full chapter, however, use only one translation, but if you read only a few verses per day, each family member can read the same verses from a different translation. This in itself has several advantages. The task of the head of the family as leader is made easier if everybody is involved and the parent doesn't have to talk all the time. Additionally, the Scripture verses are repeated several times, and the members of the family can remember them more easily and understand them better. This leads to spontaneous questions and discussion, and is therefore unforced and natural instruction of the Word. It encourages children to talk with more confidence about what they have read and understood.

Secondary sources can also be used. There are available a large number of excellent books with daily devotionals that can be read in conjunction with the Bible. We can also read sections from appropriate biographies or any spiritual literature that is edifying. In my family, we sometimes use the time over weekends to watch a spiritual film, and then discuss it and pray together. Any of the following may be applied:

- ◆ Read the Bible following a specific plan or reading programme.
- ◆ Read shorter passages from different translations of the Bible.
- ◆ Read from an appropriate children's Bible.
- ◆ Read daily devotionals, or from a Bible commentary or handbook.
- ◆ Read spiritual books and biographies.

* Watch relevant films.
* Listen to or watch a sermon video by a well-known preacher.
* Discuss the minister's sermon/s of the previous weekend.

In practice, home worship will differ from family to family. The daily programmes, routines and responsibilities of family members will have a definite impact on the practical routine of home devotions. We may not feel equipped and able to take care of the spiritual welfare of our family, but the Lord enables us to do so if we allow him to.

Do you read the Bible together? Then:

* Read according to a plan (your plan).
* Remember special events on the church calendar.
* Involve the whole family.
* Stress the importance of a personal quiet time.

When you instruct:

* Give simple, understandable explanations.
* Be sound in your theology.
* Apply truths practically.
* Be gentle and convincing.
* Get everybody's attention.
* Don't preach.

Praying

A family that prays together stays together. Families, and individual members of the family in particular, experience tremendous pressure these days. In many cases, both parents work and children are left to themselves. Families that pray together have a better chance of surviving and staying together. It is important to pray together. It serves as a practical example to children and teaches them how to pray. The quality of prayer time is more important than its length. Put before the family certain matters to pray for. This will help them in their prayers and in structuring their thoughts.

The family could pray for the following:

* personal matters and needs;

- needs of the family;
- needs of the congregation;
- the unsaved and missionaries.

And remember to give thanks for answered prayers.

OUTSTANDING DESCENDANTS

Hudson Taylor must be one of the brightest diamonds in the history of missionary work. He founded the China Inland Mission, now known as OMF International. He was only twenty-one when he first went to China. The story of his exceptional ancestors and descendants begins with his great-grandfather, who was converted on his wedding day on 1 February 1776. One of John Wesley's preachers used the words from Joshua 24:15 in the sermon at the wedding. It set James's heart on fire: 'But as for me and my house, we will serve the LORD.' He testified of his changed heart at the wedding reception. His wife was greatly shocked, but was now already married to him.

James prayed for his wife every day until she also accepted the Lord. They served the Lord together and Joshua 24:15 became their verse for life. James taught his children and grandchildren to apply this verse to their lives, too, and to serve Christ. The example of his parents and the shared times of prayer profoundly impressed the young Hudson Taylor. Every evening as he led his family devotions, Hudson Taylor's father prayed for China and the establishment of God's church there. Hudson developed an interest in missionary stories at an early age and, in particular, in stories about China. He later set out for China and established the China Inland Mission. In 1905, the church in China had grown to 100,000 members, with 800 missionaries. By 1950, the number of members had increased to 700,000 under the leadership of the China Inland Mission. Hudson had received a vision for the unsaved people of China because of his father's prayers (and his mother's devout prayers for his conversion).[26]

James Hudson Taylor V was born in 1994—the ninth generation after James Taylor. The Taylors have served the Lord as a family and have been in his service over a period of 250 years. The founding of the China Inland Mission and nine generations of Taylor descendants are the blessed fruit of a spiritual and godly family where the Lord Jesus took the place of honour and where family worship—a hidden treasure of God's blessings—was practised.[27]

The length of the prayer time depends on circumstances and the composition of the family—the number of children, their ages and their ability to concentrate. This obviously differs from family to family. In my family, we read and pray together in the evenings. We talk about needs that require prayer and then ask one member to bring a request before the Lord in prayer. If I feel that that person hasn't covered the need sufficiently, I will discuss the request again and ask the same person to pray again, or sometimes I will then pray about it.

It is useful to keep the following in mind when the family prays together:

- ◆ Pray short prayers.
- ◆ Use simple language.
- ◆ Be clear and to the point.
- ◆ Pray and talk in the same tone of voice.
- ◆ Vary your prayers.
- ◆ Confess sins when appropriate.
- ◆ Pray for others.
- ◆ Worship.

Summary

- ◆ Family worship includes joint singing.
- ◆ Family worship includes reading the Bible together.
- ◆ Family worship includes praying together.

8 What are the foundations of family worship?

Because the Christian is not his own, but bought with a price, he is to aim at glorifying God in every relation of life. No matter what station he occupies, or wherever he be, he is to serve as a witness for Christ. Next to the church of God, his own home should be the sphere of his most manifest devotedness unto Him. All its arrangements should bear the stamp of his heavenly calling. All its affairs should be so ordered that everyone entering it should feel 'God is here'.[28]

A. W. Pink

I can still remember very vividly the day when two aeroplanes flew into the World Trade Center on 11 September 2001. When it happened, I was standing next to the hospital bed of my wife after she had had an emergency operation. In November 2006, during a preaching trip to North America, my wife and I were able to visit the area, called Ground Zero, where the twin towers once stood. Several buildings alongside the North and South Tower had also been destroyed and removed. As I stood on the edge of where the buildings once were and looked down, I was simply amazed to see how deep the foundations of the buildings were. Back at our home in South Africa, we have just recently built a granny flat. The foundations for this two-storey flat were just a metre or so deep. But when I looked down into the foundations of the World Trade Center, I realized that they were probably between forty and fifty metres deep. Even the big trucks and building equipment looked like small toys from above. The size of a building, and especially its height, determines the depth of the foundation. If something is wrong with or in the foundations, it can cause severe damage to the building process or the final building itself.

If our spiritual foundations are wrong or not strong enough, the spiritual education of our families will have little or no lasting effect on the lives of our children and loved ones. They may, in fact, be deceived and misled, even though our motives may be pure. Therefore it is very important that we as parents lay proper spiritual foundations and build on them.

The command of the Lord God in Deuteronomy 11 regarding the spiritual teaching of our children is preceded by certain challenges and instructions that clearly highlight aspects of these foundations. Family worship is clearly to be built on two foundational pillars:

Love for God

We read in Deuteronomy 11:13, 'And it shall be that if you earnestly obey My commandments which I command you today, to love the Lord your God and serve Him with all your heart and with all your soul …'

Our love for the Lord is the real reason why we keep his commands. We have to love him with our whole heart and soul. What is love? Is it a feeling? Is it true love that is portrayed on television and in films? There are three different types of love:

- love for God (Greek: *agape*);
- love for a partner or spouse (*eros*);
- love for a friend (*filio*).

Love is an act of the will. Emotions and feelings are the expression of love. How do we show people that we love them? We can show it by saying good things about them or by doing good things for them. And we can show that we care by spending time with them.

Similarly, we can show God that we love him by saying good things about him, doing good things for him and spending time with him. This clearly implies a relationship and not a dead piece of theology. The proof that we really care for our loved ones is that we spend time with them, talk to them and listen to them. Our love for God is proven by the time and energy that we invest in our relationship with him.

If the personal relationship of family members with God is built on rules, regulations and barren faith, it becomes difficult and even a burden for families to keep the command of spiritual education. When it becomes an obligation and punishment, it degenerates into legalism. It is impossible for the average faithful churchgoer who doesn't have a personal love relationship with the Lord Jesus truly to take care of the spiritual education of his or her family.

If all the family members, and particularly the parents, are in an intimate love relationship with the Lord Jesus, it is so much easier—indeed, it is a joy—to pray together as a family. The members of the family then bring a tender and receptive spirit and atmosphere to the family worship. Our love relationship with the Lord Jesus is clearly evident in our daily personal quiet times, when we spend time with him as individuals through Bible reading and prayer.

Integrity and example

We read in Deuteronomy 11:16, 'Take heed to yourselves, lest your heart be deceived, and you turn aside and serve other gods and worship them.'

Love is expressed not only in spending time with our Loved One and saying good things about him, but also in doing good things for him. When we are in a love relationship, we wish to live in such a way as to make our loved one happy. It may lead to our doing things that we wouldn't normally do. It is the same in our relationship with God. We do things that we know please him. Our obedience and the protection and nurturing of our love for the Lord are the fruits of our quiet times. If we do not have a personal love relationship with him, our lives won't be true examples and lives of obedience. Even if there is a relationship, it may still be difficult to be obedient.

The result of having quiet times and a love relationship with God is a life of love, prayer, faith and obedience. It is a life of holiness and seclusion from the world, and a life dedicated to our Loved One. We wish to prepare the way for the Lord Jesus so that all mankind can see him in us (Luke 3:1–6). It is no use preaching to our children if we do exactly the opposite of what we preach. John Angell James said, 'If the parent be not visible in earnest, it cannot be expected that the child will be so.'[29]

A story of the experience of two young girls gives a striking example of how parents can have good intentions while their personal examples and characters left much to be desired. *The Teenage Marketplace* is a book written by two British teenagers. The book is based on their experiences of Western culture and society. One of the teenagers came from a very affluent family and was enrolled in a boarding school, as was the custom at that time. As a young teenager she experienced mixed feelings and emotions as she watched her parents drive away from the grounds. She started to wrestle with thoughts of death, and her father and her teachers were unable to help her.

I was mad with my parents when they lectured me about having certain standards to live up to. I couldn't understand what standards. Was it the standards of randy lords in the government who slunk off secretly to lay prostitutes and took drugs? Or were they talking about the standards I read about all the time in the press and saw on television—violence, pornography, cheating?

Perhaps it was the standards of a fashionable Boarding School with frustrating stripteases in the dormitory, yobs queuing in the lane with their filthy books and magazines for girls that treated sex like a new invention?

Deep down inside of me I was really yearning for someone I loved and respected to explain to me decisively what it all meant, what I ought to do. I know that I was not the only one. How I wish now that my parents had got hold of me, even forbidden me to leave the house on some of my stupid outings—discussed it, helping, explaining!

But why couldn't I see for myself that I was being exploited, how the pop, porn, sexy journals, TV and films, were killing my girlhood and artificially rousing my awakening sexual desires? Why can't girls see through it before they become doped or ruined? I suppose an awful lot of the adult world don't want to see through while they're cashing in.

We teenagers of all classes are reached and degraded by exploiters through discotheques, TV, pop festivals, magazines, etc. In fact I've noticed that there are probably more of the so-called privileged ones caught up in the exploiters' net. Could it be that the privileged have a less well-knit family life, due to Boarding Schools, materialism, superficial society, where no sort of adversity holds us together as a family? It is noticeable how the privileged teenagers of today search for primitive and basic things.[30]

As parents, our lives and words have to be in harmony. It needs to be possible for our children to trust us. Our lives and examples have an impact stronger than our words. Alan Redpath, a Scottish preacher and author of many books on the Christian life, explains how he became a Christian. One day, his parents had a disagreement in the house and they did not talk to each other for the whole day. As a result, they did not attend church on Sunday. But, during lunchtime, Alan's father walked into the kitchen, kneeled before his wife, took both her hands in his and asked her to forgive him for having been rude to her. All was forgiven and the atmosphere restored. Alan said, 'I was only six years old, but if that is what a Christian was, I wanted to be one.' The example of his father in the home caused him to be saved and eventually work for the Lord. We cannot preach to our children and expect them to obey if we do not live what we preach.

Summary

- Family worship may be built on wrong foundations.
- Family worship has to be grounded on the proper foundations.
- Love is an act of the will.
- Love is expressed by spending time together.
- Love is expressed by saying good things about the other.
- Love is expressed by doing good things for the other.
- Family worship is built on an intimate relationship with the Lord Jesus.
- Our lives and examples carry a message.

9 A final encouragement

As I conclude this book, I'd like to take this moment to encourage you. Preparing our families for eternity, or conducting family worship, can be rough and sometimes even very disheartening, but the blessings will be countless. The constant struggle is to find or make time to meet as a family in this fast-paced life filled with activities and responsibilities. But by persevering, we'll grow in our walk with God and experience his blessings.

One of the keys to revival in any country of the world is a revival in the home, where the Lord is worshipped and experienced daily. I am convinced that Bible-based homes are an absolute necessity for the survival and hope of our future generation and nations. Family worship is foundational in creating such Bible-based homes and new and fresh hope for the future.

Grace Crowell explains that, with God himself back in people's homes, we have hope:

> So long as there are homes to which men turn,
>   At close of day;
> So long as there are homes where children are,
>   Where women stay—
> If love and loyalty and faith be found
>   Across those sills—
> A stricken nation can recover from
>   Its gravest ills.
> So long as there are homes where fires burn,
>   And there is bread;
> So long as there are homes where lamps are lit,
>   And prayers are said—
> Although people falter through the dark,
>   And nations grope—
> With God Himself back in these homes,
>   We have sure hope.[31]

Chapter 9

I pray that I've given you some new ideas that you can begin implementing in your home immediately. I hope that you've been encouraged to believe and challenged to start with family worship and to experience all the blessings that the Lord intends for you as a family to experience. He promises to bless you, multiply the days of your lives, drive out the enemies before you and even give you all the ground that you march over. We read:

> ... that your days and the days of your children may be multiplied in the land of which the LORD swore to your fathers to give them, like the days of the heavens above the earth. 'For if you carefully keep all these commandments which I command you to do—to love the LORD your God, to walk in all His ways, and to hold fast to Him—then the LORD will drive out all these nations from before you, and you will dispossess greater and mightier nations than yourselves. Every place on which the sole of your foot treads shall be yours: from the wilderness and Lebanon, from the river, the River Euphrates, even to the Western Sea, shall be your territory. No man shall be able to stand against you; the LORD your God will put the dread of you and the fear of you upon all the land where you tread, just as He has said to you.
>
> Deut. 11:21–25

Just think about that: God promised that he would become personally involved with his people if they kept his commandments and served him wholeheartedly. Will you join me in seeking him for this blessing?

Heavenly Father, help us to understand that Christian homes are built systematically and daily as we walk with you. Lord, help us to seek your face together each day in our homes and teach your Word to our children when we rise up and when we lie down. When we sit in our homes and walk by the way, may they hear us speak the blessings of God. We commit our families and homes to you and to your service. Help us to worship you daily in our homes. In the name of Jesus Christ, our Saviour and Lord. Amen.

Appendix 1: Where do I start?

Perhaps you have read this book and now realize for the first time the importance and value of family worship. You also realize that you do not have a choice as to whether or not to obey this command of the Lord. Perhaps you stand accused and convicted because of the lack of spiritual guidance and education of your family, and you feel guilty about it.

The following thoughts may enter your mind: 'I did take the children to church on Sundays to attend Sunday school. I sent them to various church camps. We attended church every Sunday morning and even went to some special meetings at church. Aren't those things enough? Why do I then feel so guilty? I realize that I have to give spiritual guidance at home—but where do I start? I cannot pray out loud. I have no training. I don't even know if I am right with the Lord.'

I have exceptionally good news for you: you don't have to start anywhere, because the Lord Jesus has already started for you. The very fact that you are feeling guilty and are convicted of the need to do something about it is proof enough. The Lord Jesus is already working in your heart through his Holy Spirit. Therefore, he has already started. All you need to do is to allow him to continue his work in you, and work with him. He will assist you. He will also prepare the way in the hearts and lives of your loved ones.

You can follow these simple steps:

Step 1. Pray about worshipping as a family
Before implementing family worship, it is important to think about all the aspects and to pray about the matter. Retreat into your study or any other quiet place where you can be with the Lord in solitude. Then:

- Pray.
- Confess the sin of your disobedience to the command of the Lord regarding family worship.

- Confess your sin of negligence in not guiding your family spiritually.
- Confess any other intentional sin that occurs in your home.
- Confess the sins that you have allowed and even participated in.
- Be honest and sincere; don't vindicate yourself.
- Ask God for forgiveness. Experience his forgiveness.
- Ask for his advice and wisdom.
- Ask for his guidance and help in the implementation of family worship.

Step 2. Focus on yourself

It is of the utmost importance that you, as head of the family and initiator of family worship, should be right with God. Ensure that you have perfect peace in your heart regarding your personal relationship with the Lord Jesus. You should be 100 per cent certain of your faith in God and know that you are right with God (1 John 5:13). Set up an appointment with a spiritual mentor to discuss the certainty of faith if you have any doubts or questions.

Start the discipline of having a daily personal quiet time with God. Get up a little earlier in the morning. Go to your quiet place of worship to spend time with the Lord. Read from his Word, read from devotionals or other spiritual literature, and pray. Pray for yourself and for your family. Have intimate communion with the Lord.

Ask the Lord Jesus to show you if there is anything in your life that saddens and hurts him. If the Lord reveals such things to you through his Spirit:

- Confess these things honestly to the Lord Jesus.
- Ask for and receive his forgiveness.
- Make restitution if necessary.
- If required, break with the sin or the pattern of behaviour.

If the Lord Jesus reveals to you that you are guilty before a member of your family:

- Confess it honestly to the Lord Jesus.
- Ask for and receive his forgiveness.

- Ask your loved one to forgive you.
- Break with that sin or pattern of behaviour.

Step 3. Plan a family meeting

You are excited but at the same time probably apprehensive. In fact, you do not know how to start. It is important not to bombard the family spiritually, especially not the children. Be wise and instead opt for bringing the family together for an informal meeting. Plan an excursion, a meal in a restaurant or simply coffee on the patio.

Explain to your family that it is important to get together from time to time to give all family members an opportunity to discuss topics that are important to them. Each family member can bring up what he or she wants to discuss. Compile a discussion list. You can start by discussing those less important matters that nevertheless form part of the daily activity of the family. The following are examples of topics that lend themselves to discussion:

- the yearly family holiday;
- a special weekend away for the parents;
- a family evening;
- the children's spending money;
- the tasks and responsibilities of every family member;
- and, of course, family worship.

Step 4. Discuss the necessity of family worship

You could start by telling your family that you have read this book and share the impact it had on you. You are convinced of the importance of the family reading and praying together, but the family has to decide how, where and when this should take place. You could even give a copy of the book to all the family members and ask them to read it. Plan a follow-up family meeting where you will make decisions about the format of family worship. While you wait for the next meeting:

- Be faithful and consistent with your daily quiet times.
- Pray every day for your family.
- Live an exemplary life at home.
- Support your loved ones.

Step 5. Follow-up family meeting

Over and above family worship you can add new points to the agenda if all the other matters have already been dealt with. Discuss what you have read in this book on family worship and how it can be applied within the routine of the family. Take care to include the following:

- what each member expects of family worship;
- where it should take place;
- when it should take place;
- what will be done during a family worship session;
- how it will be carried out;
- when your first meeting to pray together as a family will take place.

Appendix 2: Suggested format for family worship using the Bible

Step 1. Your preparation

As a family, you have now decided what you are going to do and where you are going to meet. You have decided to read a few verses from a specific book in the Bible during your family worship. As soon as you have finished that Bible book, the family will decide which book to read next.

It is very important to prepare for the family worship. Remember that this preparation *does not replace* your personal quiet time. In preparation, you can do the following:

- Pray and ask the Lord to show you what is in his heart.
- Read the appropriate verses from the Bible.
- Read about the background of the chosen verses—from a commentary or concordance if necessary.
- Ask yourself questions, such as: What is the meaning of this passage? What does the Lord wish to say? What does he expect of me? Apply the answers to your life.
- Pray for your presentation of the family worship. Pray for: wisdom and insight; confidence to lead; a warm and informal atmosphere; the Lord's presence; that his will will be done.

This will ensure that you reap the following benefits:

- the creation of a devout atmosphere;
- the retention of proper focus;
- the family worship will be presented systematically;
- there will be confirmation of your spiritual leadership;
- you will be prepared to answer any questions.

Step 2. Welcome

Greet all the members of the family. Sometimes it may be necessary to allow time for members to share happenings from their day and problems or crises that they are experiencing at that point in time. This offers an opportunity to unload stress and tension, and from this there may also flow prayer requests that can be dealt with later. The sharing of thoughts binds the family together and awakens a feeling of solidarity. Do not spend too much time on this; allow sufficient time for reading and praying together. Be very sensitive at all times to the leading and prompting of the Holy Spirit.

Step 3. Open with prayer

Open with a prayer. You could pray yourself or you could ask someone else to commit the family worship to the Lord. Allow time for silent prayers. Thus your thoughts are focused on the Lord and the time that you want to spend with him. You will again become conscious of his presence through his Spirit.

Step 4. Read from the Bible

The family has agreed to read a certain section, chapter or book from the Bible. Read the appropriate Scripture. It is important to read according to a plan and not simply leaf through the Bible. Choose a Bible in accordance with the age of your children. For younger children, use a children's Bible. It is also important that you, as head of the family, do the reading.

Step 5. Read from different translations

Ask members of your family to read the same passage in their own Bibles and from other translations of the Bible. If the children are small, omit this step.

Step 6. Discussion

It isn't always necessary to discuss, explain or study the Scripture reading. Reading different translations often clarifies it sufficiently. It is important, however, to offer the opportunity for every member of the family to react to the reading. You can ask them what they heard and what they understood. In this way you ensure that they have understood and grasped what has been read.

Ask the following questions:

+ What is the meaning of this piece of Scripture?
+ What does the Lord wish to say?

◆ What does he expect of us?

Step 7. Personal and practical application
Discuss and explain how the Scripture reading applies to your daily programme and routine. Let every family member share how he or she can apply it personally. It is important to close the Scripture reading with a personal challenge and a practical application.

Step 8. Prayer time
The family should determine the length of the prayer time and even who has to pray. This may lessen potential tension or stress. If family members do not feel confident to pray out loud, allow time for silent prayers. Ask for specific prayer requests or pray for matters that were mentioned at the start of the meeting. You could give the opportunity for prayer to only one member of the family, or you could allow time for more prayers.

Step 9. Joint singing
Close your family worship by singing a fitting and well-known song in a way that your family is comfortable with.

Step 10. Obedience
It may happen that the Lord Jesus speaks to you or one of the family members and that he requires an act of obedience in faith. Emphasize the importance of obedience and take the necessary action. If you have to ask for forgiveness from one of the family members or confess a sin, do it.

Appendix 3: Suggested format for family worship using the Bible and a devotional diar

Step 1. Your preparation

As a family you have now decided what you are going to do and where you are going to meet. You have decided to read a book with daily devotionals alongside the Bible during your family worship. As soon as you have finished that book, the family will decide which book to read next.

It is very important to prepare for the family worship. Remember that this preparation *does not replace* your personal quiet time. In preparation, you can do the following:

- Pray and ask the Lord to show you what is in his heart.
- Read the appropriate verses from the Bible.
- Read about the background of the chosen verses—from a commentary or concordance if necessary.
- Ask yourself questions, such as: What is the meaning of this passage? What does the Lord wish to say? What does he expect of me? Apply the answers to your life.
- Pray for your presentation of the family worship. Pray for: wisdom and insight; confidence to lead; a warm and informal atmosphere; the Lord's presence; that his will will be done.

This will ensure that you reap the following benefits:

- the creation of a devout atmosphere;
- the retention of proper focus;
- the family worship will be presented systematically;
- there will be confirmation of your spiritual leadership;
- you will be prepared to answer any questions.

Step 2. Welcome

Greet all the members of the family. Sometimes it may be necessary to allow time for members to share happenings from their day and problems or crises that they are experiencing at that point in time. This offers an opportunity to unload stress and tension, and from this there may also flow prayer requests that can be dealt with later. The sharing of thoughts binds the family together and awakens a feeling of solidarity. Do not spend too much time on this; allow sufficient time for reading and praying together. Be very sensitive at all times to the leading and prompting of the Holy Spirit.

Step 3. Open with prayer

Open with a prayer. You could pray yourself or you could ask someone else to commit the family worship to the Lord. Allow time for silent prayers. Thus your thoughts are focused on the Lord and the time that you want to spend with him. You will again become conscious of his presence through his Spirit.

Step 4. Read from the Bible

The family has agreed to use a specific devotional diary alongside the Bible. Read the Scripture listed for that day in the devotional. Choose a Bible in accordance with the age of your children. For younger children, use a children's Bible. It is also important that you, as head of the family, do the reading.

Step 5. Read the devotional

Now read the relevant piece for the day from your devotional diary.

Step 6. Discussion

It isn't always necessary to discuss, explain or study the Scripture reading. Reading different translations often clarifies it sufficiently. It is important, however, to offer the opportunity for every member of the family to react to the reading. You can ask them what they heard and what they understood. In this way you ensure that they have understood and grasped what has been read.

Ask the following questions:

- ◆ What is the meaning of this piece of Scripture?
- ◆ What does the Lord wish to say?
- ◆ What does he expect of us?

Step 7. Personal and practical application

Discuss and explain how the Scripture reading applies to your daily programme and routine. Let every family member share how he or she can apply it personally. It is important to close the Scripture reading with a personal challenge and a practical application.

Step 8. Prayer time

The family should determine the length of the prayer time and even who has to pray. This may lessen potential tension or stress. If family members do not feel confident to pray out loud, allow time for silent prayers. Ask for specific prayer requests or pray for matters that were mentioned at the start of the meeting. You could give the opportunity for prayer to only one member of the family, or you could allow time for more prayers.

Step 9. Joint singing

Close your family worship by singing a fitting and well-known song in a way that your family is comfortable with.

Step 10. Obedience

It may happen that the Lord Jesus speaks to you or one of the family members and that he requires an act of obedience in faith. Emphasize the importance of obedience and take the necessary action. If you have to ask for forgiveness from one of the family members or confess a sin, do it.

Appendix 4: An example of family worship

Step 1. Welcome

Hello, everybody. It's been a long day, but it is so good to be together, especially when our purpose is to spend some time with the Lord and his lovely presence.

Would anyone like to share anything? You may talk about whatever you want to. Perhaps you wish to share what you have experienced and applied practically since last night's family worship. Or have you encountered any problems or met with difficulties that we can pray about tonight? And to each of you: please share what you have learnt in your personal quiet time.

(Listen to the testimonies, remarks and reports of your family. Agree with what they raise. If the subject has general relevance, make a note to return to it and to pray about it. If it concerns only one person, jot it down and talk to the family member after the worship in order to support and advise him or her.)

Step 2. Open with prayer

Let us pray together: Lord Jesus, thank you for the wonderful privilege that we can come together as a family in your name. Thank you for protecting us today and bringing us together safely. Thank you that we know that you are here with us as you promised in your Word. Come and speak to each one of us tonight in such a way that we may understand what you want to tell us. Amen.

Step 3. Read from the Bible

Rachel, will you please read John 15:1–7. *(We all follow in our own Bibles while Rachel reads from the translation of her choice.)*

Step 4. Read the devotional from the diary

Thank you. The title for today is 'Remain in him'. *(You read the section slowly and clearly.)*

Step 5. Discussion

Does anybody want to comment on the Scripture verses or the piece that I have just read? *(Listen to the testimonies, remarks and reports from your family. Agree with what they mention. Ensure that everybody understands all that has been discussed.)*

Step 6. Personal and practical application

What is the meaning of this Scripture? What does the Lord wish to say? What does he expect of us?

How do we remain in Jesus? We remain in him by spending time with him, reading his Word and praying. Furthermore, we stay in him by obeying him. Remember to have your personal quiet time every day and to read the Bible and pray daily. Don't skip a day.

Step 7. Prayer

Good, let's pray together. Whose turn is it tonight? Rachel! Are there any prayer requests? *(Rachel includes all the requests in her prayer.)*

Step 8. Joint singing

Let's close by singing a song. Any suggestions? Right, let's sing Psalm 23. *(We all sing Psalm 23.)*

Closing

Remember to read your Bible every day and not to skip your personal quiet time. Our family worship should not take the place of your own love-relationship with the Lord Jesus.

Whose turn is it to make us a nice cup of coffee?

Select bibliography

Alexander, J. W., *Thoughts on Family Worship* (Morgan, PA: Soli Deo Gloria, 1990).

Beeke, Joel, *Family Worship* (Grand Rapids, MI: Reformation Heritage Books, 2002).

Blackaby, Henry, *Chosen to be God's Prophet* (Nashville, TN: Thomas Nelson, 2003).

Bounds, E. M., *Krag deur Gebed* (Kempton Park, South Africa: Heart-Publishers, 1973).

Carr, Francois, *My Time with Him* (Pretoria, South Africa: Te Deum, 2004).

Cromarty, Jim, *King of the Cannibals* (Auburn, MA: Evangelical Press, 1997).

Evans, Eifion, *The Welsh Revival of 1904* (Bridgend: Evangelical Press of Wales, 1969).

Harvey, Edwin and Lillian, *How They Prayed*, vol. i: *Household Prayers* (Hampton, TN: Harvey and Tait, 1987).

Marcellino, Jerry, *Rediscovering the Lost Treasure of Family Worship* (Laurel, MS: Audubon Press, 2002).

McCheyne, Robert Murray, *The Deeper Life* (Wheaton, IL: World Wide Publications, 1994).

Ryken, Leland, *Worldly Saints* (Grand Rapids, MI: Zondervan, 1986).

Ryle, J. C., *The Duties of Parents* (Conrad, MT: Triangle Press, 1993).

Stewart, James Alexander, *She Was Only 22* (Asheville, NC: Revival Literature, 2004).

Taylor 111, James Hudson, *God's Grace to Nine Generations* (Singapore: OMF Publishing, 1999).

Endnotes

1 Quoted in Edwin and Lillian Harvey, *How They Prayed*, vol. i: *Household Prayers* (Hampton, TN: Harvey and Tait, 1987), p. 9.

2 Ibid., p. 14.

3 Quoted in James Stewart, *She Was Only 22* (Asheville, NC: Revival Literature, 2004), p. 5.

4 Ibid.

5 Ibid., p. 122.

6 Leonard Ravenhill, *Why Revival Tarries* (Minneapolis, MN: Sovereign World/Bethany House, 1959), p. 157.

7 Harvey, *How They Prayed*, pp. 15–16.

8 Quoted in Jerry Marcellino, *Rediscovering the Lost Treasure of Family Worship* (Laurel, MS: Audubon Press, 2002), p. 20.

9 See Eifion Evans, *The Welsh Revival of 1904* (Bridgend: Evangelical Press of Wales, 1969).

10 Quoted in Richard Owen Roberts (ed.), *Sanctify the Congregation* (Wheaton, IL: International Awakening Press, 1994), p. 24.

11 *Decision Magazine* (Billy Graham Evangelistic Association), May 2007, pp. 26–34.

12 Quoted in Joel Beeke, *Family Worship* (Grand Rapids, MI: Reformation and Heritage Books, 2002), p. 25.

13 Quoted in James Kennedy, *The Secret to a Happy Home* (New Kensington, PA: Whitaker House, 1987), p. 169.

14 Leland Ryken, *Worldly Saints* (Grand Rapids, MI: Zondervan, 1986), p. 74.

15 J. C. Ryle, *The Duties of Parents* (Conrad, MT: Triangle Press, 1993).

16 Marcellino, *Rediscovering the Lost Treasure of Family Worship*, p. 8.

17 James W. Alexander, *Thoughts on Family Worship* (Morgan, PA: Soli Deo Gloria, 1990), pp. 1–2.

18 Dr Henry Blackaby, *Chosen to be God's Prophet* (Nashville, TN: Thomas Nelson, 2003).

19 Quoted in Ryken, *Worldly Saints*, p. 73.

20 Quoted in Beeke, *Family Worship*, p. 22.

21 Alexander, *Thoughts on Family Worship*, pp. 1–2.

22 Ibid. [page not known].

23 Quoted in Marcellino, *Rediscovering the Lost Treasure of Family Worship*, p. 18.

24 Terry L. Johnson, *The Family Worship Book* (Fearn: Christian Focus, 1998), p. 18.

25 See Jim Cromarty, *King of the Cannibals* (Auburn, MA: Evangelical Press, 1997).

26 Jim Cromarty, *The Pigtail and Chopsticks Man* (Darlington: Evangelical Press, 2002), pp. 35–40.

27 See James Hudson Taylor III, *God's Grace to Nine Generations* (Singapore: OMF Publishing, 1999).

28 Quoted in Marcellino, *Rediscovering the Lost Treasure of Family Worship*, p. 18.

29 Quoted in Ryken, *Worldly Saints*, p. 23.

30 Quoted in Harvey, *How They Prayed*, pp. 11–14.

31 Quoted in Harvey, *How They Prayed*, pp. 9–10.

ABOUT DAY ONE:

Day One's threefold commitment:
- To be faithful to the Bible, God's inerrant, infallible Word;
- To be relevant to our modern generation;
- To be excellent in our publication standards.

I continue to be thankful for the publications of Day One. They are biblical; they have sound theology; and they are relevant to the issues at hand. The material is condensed and manageable while, at the same time, being complete—a challenging balance to find. We are happy in our ministry to make use of these excellent publications.

JOHN MACARTHUR, PASTOR-TEACHER, GRACE COMMUNITY CHURCH, CALIFORNIA

It is a great encouragement to see Day One making such excellent progress. Their publications are always biblical, accessible and attractively produced, with no compromise on quality. Long may their progress continue and increase!

JOHN BLANCHARD, AUTHOR, EVANGELIST AND APOLOGIST

Visit our web site for more information and
to request a free catalogue of our books.

www.dayone.co.uk

Also available

Teach your family the Truth
Building on the basics of the Faith

BRIAN STONE

ISBN 978-1-84625-129-0

128PP, PAPERBACK

God's Word is a lamp to our feet and a light to our path, and we are always looking for tools to assist us in becoming more effective in our study and application of the Scriptures. This is what this book is intended to be—a building block in the basics of the faith, in assisting parents to train up their children in the ways of the Lord, in the context of family devotions.

It is also intended to be used by older children as a tool to assist them in coming to understand the riches of the wonderful truths that are to be found in the Word of God.

'Catechising imaginatively, vivaciously and spiritually is a superlative means of grace available for all Christian families. I love the way Brian Stone has put this one together and commend it highly.'

ERROLL HULSE, EDITOR, REFORMATION TODAY

'I am very pleased that Brian Stone has written this catechism. It has long been needed. Every family should own one in order to improve family worship.'

JOHN TEMPLE, FATHER OF FOUR AND GRANDFATHER TO FOURTEEN

'Baptists have a rich heritage of using catechisms to instruct children and new believers. I am delighted that recent years have witnessed a recovery of that heritage. This work by Brian Stone will be a wonderful blessing to parents and children alike who follow its user-friendly plan.'

TOM ASCOL, EXECUTIVE DIRECTOR OF FOUNDERS MINISTRIES, PASTOR OF GRACE BAPTIST CHURCH, CAPE CORAL, FLORIDA, USA

FOCAL POINT

Lead your family in worship

Discovering the enjoyment of God

All churches want to experience growth. Many churches are implementing special projects and techniques in order to achieve this growth. But churches consist of families—and families consist of individuals. If a family is spiritually healthy, this leads to spontaneous growth in the church and to the spiritual development of the community. Yet few churches focus their growth, particularly their spiritual growth, on the foundation of the holiness of individuals and family members. The traditional practice of family worship has become neglected as a result.

Here Francois Carr pleads for the return of family worship times. What is family worship? Why is it so rarely practised today? What should a family worship time consist of? How can my family get started? Illustrated with examples of many great men and women in church history, this book answers these questions and demonstrates the influence for good that the practice of family worship has had down through the centuries. Appendixes are included as examples of family worship sessions in action.

This helpful work will be a great help to tho parents seeking to build homes that honour

—*Dr Richard Blackaby, Director of Blackaby Ministries, Canada*

Read and pray over its contents. The Lord ca use it to bless your family and also your chur I commend this little book to you.

—*Dr Eryl Davies, Former Principal, Evangelic Theological College of Wales, United Kingdo*

Francois Carr instructs most helpfully in grea practical detail how each family can begin worship together in the home.

—*Dr Colin Peckham, Former Principal, Faith Mission Bible School, Edinburgh, Scotland*

Francois Carr B. Th., M.C.C., D. Min., NDPB is currently the Executi Director both of Reviva South Africa and Te De Ministries. He is the se editor of *Revival, A Journal On Prayer, Holiness and Revival.* He is co-sponsor of the Heart Cry Conferences in the USA Malawi and South Africa. He is also the author of several books. He is a popula conference speaker in the USA, UK, Euro and several countries in Africa. Francois married to Dorothea and they have one daughter, Leoné.

Day One Publications
Ryelands Road Leominster HR6 8NZ
Email: sales@dayone.co.uk | www.dayone.co.uk
☏ +44 (0) 1568 613 740 | FAX 01568 611 473
☏ Toll Free 888 329 6630 (North America)

£ 4.00

DayOne.

ISBN: 978-1846251283

£5

9 781846 251283 >